Business English Now!

Alex Timberman 지음

Business English Now!

2015년 2월 10일 초판 인쇄
2015년 2월 25일 초판 발행

지은이 Alex Timberman
고문 설성수
발행인 배효선
발행처 법문사
등록 1957년 12월 12일 / 제2-76호(윤)
주소 경기도 파주시 회동길 37-29 (문발동)
전화 031-955-6500 **Fax** 031-955-6525
홈페이지 www.bobmunsa.co.kr

한글 교열 안종대 이강직 조우리
디자인 Design by Design Maum
책편집 이지현

Design by Mauem Designs
Translation by Bob Jong Dae Ahn and Kangjik Lee, Woo Ree Jo

Inquires to the author should be addressed to: timbermanalex@gmail.com

For Bobby

Author's Introduction

작가소개

Alex Timberman spent most of his life in the Southern U.S. state of Arkansas. A place famous for Bill Clinton, Douglas MacArthur, and the retail giant Wal-Mart. After having been a successful business owner, unsuccessful stock trader, and a licensed but unpracticed lawyer, he decided to try his luck and adventure in South Korea.

He arrived in South Korea to find an obsession over English. To help prepare his students for a job-market that prefers English speakers, he decided to write this book.

It's difficult for students to understand why they have to speak English when most of the workforce is mainly Korean, so he decided to write a book on business and on getting a job that will allow them to sharpen their conversation skills in a fun way. He believes everyone has the potential to speak English well enough to conduct business with anyone, anywhere, anytime.

If you are working at a university and would like the set of PowerPoints that go along with the book, or if you need to contact the author with questions, please email to timbermanalex@gmail.com

Alex Timberman은 Bill Clinton, Douglas MacArthur, 거대 기업인 Wal-Mart로 유명한 Arkansas 주에서 생의 대부분을 보냈습니다. 그는 성공적인 기업오너로서, 또 성공적이지 못한 주식거래자로서, 자격은 있으나 현장경험이 없는 변호사로 지낸 후, 자신의 운과 모험을 한국에서 걸어보기로 결정했습니다.

한국에 온 그는 한국이 영어에 대한 강박관념을 가지고 있다는 것을 알게 됩니다. 영어로 말할 수 있는 사람을 더 선호하는 취업시장에서 취업 준비생들을 돕기 위해, 이 책을 쓰기로 하였습니다.

전 직원 대부분이 한국인임에도 불구하고, 왜 영어를 사용하는지에 대해 학생들이 이해하기 곤란해하자, 그는 재미있는 방식으로 대화 기술을 갈고 닦을 수 있는 비지니스와 취업에 관한 책을 쓰기로 결정합니다. 그는 모든 사람들이 영어를 어떤 누구와 어디서건, 어느 때건, 사업 수행을 할 수 있을 정도로 충분히 잘할 수 있는 잠재력이 있다고 믿고 있습니다.

만약 대학에서 근무 중이시거나 이 책에 딸린 파워포인트를 원하는 경우, 질문은 timbermanalex@gmail.com으로 메일을 보내주시기 바랍니다.

About the Book

Like it or not, English is the global language of business. Many companies in Korea look for workers who are able to facilitate communication on a global scale. This book helps the university student to sharpen their conversational skills on general business topics such as preparing for a job, doing well at work, and on topics like the economy and society that extend beyond work.

This book is for business students at the university level. Many books focus on irrelevant topics or lack questions that evoke provocative and thought-provoking ideas. This book is suitable for the university semester schedule and can be finished by completing one to two units per week. It focuses on intermediate vocabulary and idioms; however, the main focus is on speaking but without the unnatural dialogs or drills that you find in many other texts. It is written for the instructor who can encourage conversation using the contents of each unit, explaining the words in different contexts.

Even though the book is for intermediate level, our experience is that many classes have students at varying levels. Thus, the instructor should challenge lower level students but at the same time expand on the discussion to engage higher level students. Feel free to add presentations or essay assignments to suit the class needs. Personalized tests can be made using the discussion questions and vocabulary. And if a topic is interesting, take your time with a longer lesson. Just know that the book was written with you in mind for you to carry out an interesting class in an organized way.

In addition, the vocabulary, idioms, and discussion questions have been minimally translated into Korean to ensure interest and understanding while the exercises are designed to expand vocabulary by the study of synonyms and antonyms. Moreover, students can improve their writing and demonstrate their mastery of the vocabulary and idioms by creating their own sentences. We hope that the topic selection of the chapters, the translation into Korean, and the provocative discussion questions from each chapter helps you to lead an interesting class every time.

좋든 싫든, 영어는 전 세계 업무용 언어입니다. 한국 내의 많은 기업들이 세계적 규모로 의사소통이 가능한 사람을 찾고 있습니다. 이 책은 업무 활동을 넘어서 경제, 사회와 같은 주제를 원활히 다루거나 사무를 잘 하거나 구직활동과 같은 일반적인 비즈니스 주제에 대한 대학생들의 대화 실력을 연마할 수 있도록 도와 주는 책입니다.

이 책은 대학교 수준의 학생들에게 알맞은 책입니다. 많은 책들이 관계없는 주제에 초점을 맞추거나 자극적이고 진지하게 생각할 아이디어를 떠올리는 질문이 부족합니다. 이 책은 대학교 학기 일정에 알맞으며 한 주에 1~2 단원씩 진도를 나간다면 마칠 수 있을 것입니다. 이 책은 중급 단어와 숙어에 초점을 맞추고 있습니다; 그렇지만 다른 많은 교재에서 보여지는 부자연스럽거나 반복된 대화들은 없으며, 말하기에 집중되어 있습니다. 이 책은 각 본문에 있는 내용을 가지고 단어들을 서로 다른 맥락에서 설명하고 회화를 독려할 수 있는 강사를 위하여 쓰여졌습니다.

이 책이 중급 레벨이지만 우리 경험상 많은 강의실의 학생들의 수준은 서로 많이 다릅니다. 따라서, 강사는 낮은 수준의 학생들을 도전하게 하는 동시에 논의를 확대시켜 높은 수준의 학생들을 사로잡아야 합니다. 수업의 필요에 맞게 자유롭게 발표나 작문 과제를 부여해도 좋습니다. 대화문제나 단어를 이용하여 맞춤형 시험을 만들 수도 있습니다. 그리고 만약 주제가 흥미롭다면, 천천히 좀더 오래 강의하면 됩니다. 이 책은 조직화된 방법으로 흥미로운 수업을 하기 위한 강사들을 염두에 두고 쓰여진 책이라는 것을 유념해 주시기 바랍니다.

이에 더하여, 이 책은 동의어와 반의어의 학습을 통하여 영어의 어휘 능력을 확장시키는 연습을 할 수 있도록 구성이 짜여 있으며 동시에 단어, 관용어구, 토론 질문은 최소한의 한국어 번역이 되어 있어 독자들이 내용을 확실하게 이해할 수 있게 하고 흥미를 갖게 합니다. 더군다나 학생들은 스스로 영어 문장을 만들어 봄으로써 글 쓰기 실력을 향상시킬 수 있고, 어휘와 관용어구를 통달할 수도 있습니다. 챕터들의 선별된 주제와 한국어 번역문과 각 챕터마다 있는 흥미로운 질문들이 수업을 재미있게 이끌어 가는 데 도움이 되기를 바랍니다.

복사는 작가의 시간과 노력을 경시하는 것입니다. 교사들이 책의 무단 복사를 하지 않는 것이 저자의 희망입니다. 또한, 책의 깨끗한 사본은 교사의 보다 전문적인 표시가 될 뿐만 아니라 깨끗한 책을 소지하는 것은 모든 학기에 책을 사용하는 학생들에게 좋은 인상을 남깁니다. 마지막으로, 이 책에 사용된 사진은 크리에이티브 커먼즈 라이센스의 저작권법에 의해 허용된 것입니다.

2015. 2

Alex Timberman

How to Use the Book

Speaking tests such as OPIC, TOEIC speaking, and IELTS use pronunciation, intonation, grammar, vocabulary, and logic as criteria. Therefore, we hope that conversation practice considers the evaluation criteria of different tests, while being fun in itself. The suggestions that follow are advice on how to improve the conversation of students in general and for the various speaking tests out there, but the teacher should use their expertise and discretion to carry out the lessons in a way that best match teacher's style with student's interests.

STEP • 01 Reading the chapter

To correct pronunciation and intonation, it is recommended that the teacher either allows the students to repeat the teacher sentence by sentence while reading the chapter or for teachers to correct the students after they read each sentence or paragraph. Whether students read out loud the sentence or paragraph may depend on the class size. Large classes can work with one student reading one sentence followed by immediate corrections and smaller classes can work on a paragraph-by-paragraph basis.

STEP • 02 Key vocabulary and phrases

Teachers using this book can use the accompanying PowerPoints slides to the chapters or create their own. These PowerPoint slides either allows students to finish a sentence using the key vocabulary word, or just provide a definition of the word. Here, teachers should check to see whether the students can understand the word and provide further example sentences or explanations as necessary.

STEP • 03

Conversation questions

Students should form into groups of 2,3,4, or 5. Each group size should depend on the dynamics of the class. To avoid terse and sparse answers, teachers should set standards for students to answer each question for at least 1 minute. Moreover, students should be encouraged to "dance" around the questions, meaning to ask follow up questions when curious or to segue into related discussions as in a real conversation. Besides, students should be taught the basics of answering a question with logic: using a useful introductory clause, getting to the main point, and finishing with the appropriate concluding sentence.

STEP • 04

Exercises and writing

If time allows, teachers can correct the writing of students' homework. In addition, teachers can assign group or individual presentations either using the conversation questions or from some of the suggested assignments related to some chapters. The objective of the exercises is to help students to reinforce what they have learned by completing exercises and by incorporating what they have learned for use in their own writing or presentation.

이 책의 사용법

OPIC, TOEIC speaking, IELTS와 같은 말하기 테스트에서는 발음, 억양, 문법, 어휘, 논리를 평가 기준으로 하고 있습니다. 그래서 우리는 대화 연습이 다양한 테스트의 평가 기준을 고려하는 동시에 그 자체로서도 재미있기를 바랍니다. 다음과 같은 제안은 일반적인 학생들의 말하기 능력을 향상시키는 방법과 다양한 말하기 테스트를 대비한 조언이지만, 선생님들은 자신들의 스타일과 학생들의 흥미를 가장 잘 조화시킬 수 있도록 전문지식과 재량을 발휘해야 합니다.

단계 • 01

챕터 읽기

발음과 억양을 교정하기 위해서는 학생들이 한 문장 한 문장 선생님을 따라 읽거나 학생이 문장이나 문단을 읽은 다음, 선생님이 직접 학생들을 교정해 주는 것을 권장합니다. 학생들이 문장이나 문단을 크게 읽을지는 반의 크기에 따라 달라질 수 있습니다. 규모가 큰 반의 경우 한 학생마다 한 문장을 읽고 바로 수정할 수 있고, 그보다 작은 규모에서는 문단 기준으로 할 수 있을 것입니다.

단계 • 02

주요 어휘 및 구문

이 책을 사용하는 선생님은 함께 있는 파워 포인트 슬라이드를 각 챕터에 맞게 사용하거나 직접 만들 수 있습니다. 이 파워포인트 슬라이드는 학생들이 주요한 어휘 및 단어를 사용하여 문장을 만들 수 있도록 도와 주거나 단순히 단어의 정의 만을 제공할 수도 있습니다. 여기서, 선생님들은 학생들이 그 단어를 이해할 수 있는지를 확인하여야 하며 필요한 경우 더 많은 예문과 설명을 제공하여야 할 것입니다.

단계 • 03

대화 질문

학생들은 각각 2, 3, 4, 또는 5명의 그룹을 만듭니다. 그룹의 규모는 수업의 강약에 따라 달라집니다. 너무 짧거나 빈약한 대답을 피하기 위해, 선생님들은 학생들이 최소한 1분 동안 각 질문에 대해 대답할 수 있는 기준을 마련해야 합니다. 더하여, 학생들은 질문들 주위를 "춤추도록" 고무되어야 합니다. 이는 실제 대화에서처럼 호기심에 계속 질문을 한다든가, 연관된 토론으로 넘어가기 위해 질문을 한다든가 하는 것입니다. 또한 학생들은 논리적으로 질문에 답하는 기본을 배워야 합니다. 즉, 시작하는 문장, 요점, 적절한 결론으로 마무리하기입니다.

단계 • 04

연습과 쓰기

만일 시간이 허락된다면, 선생님들은 학생들이 집에서 해온 쓰기 숙제를 교정할 수 있을 것입니다. 게다가, 그룹이나 개인별로 대화 질문을 사용하거나 몇몇 챕터와 연관성이 있는 제안 과제를 사용하여 발표를 맡길 수도 있을 것입니다. 이 연습의 목적은 학생들이 이를 마치며 그리고 쓰기나 발표에서 사용하기 위해 배운 것을 종합하며, 배운 내용을 더 강화할 수 있도록 도울 것입니다.

Table of Contents

Module 03. Thinking beyond work 일 그 이상의 생각

Module 01.

Preparing for work 취업준비하기

Unit 01

Setting Goals

Motivator Tony Robbins once said, "Setting goals is the first step in turning the invisible into the visible." Of course, everyone has different aims, desires, and goals. Some have long-term goals such as getting a good job, getting married, or traveling the world. Others have short-term goals, such as acing a test, finishing a marathon, or starting a new hobby.

Whether short term or long term, having a goal helps you take action toward whatever it is that you really want. Without goals, you may not progress despite an ardent desire to somehow succeed. The first thing you should do is to ponder over what is important for your life. Then you should accept the fact that you will have to overcome some obstacles along the way. There are no ifs and buts about it. Some sacrifices have to be made.

Just don't bite off more than you can chew. However, aim for the sky following some strategy to achieve your goals. One strategy is the SMART method, which stands for specific, measurable, attainable, realistic, and time-bound. Being specific will make your goals unambiguous and measuring your goals will ensure that you see the progress. By setting yourself goals that are attainable, you can figure out how to actually accomplish your aim instead of just dreaming about it. In addition, ensure that your goals are relevant because you do not want to waste your time. After all, time is money, so ensure that your goals are time-bound ones so that you have some sense of urgency to achieve your goals within a reasonable target date.

- Key Vocabulary
- Idioms and Expressions

해석

목표설정

동기부여자 토니 로빈스는 "목표를 설정하는 것은 볼 수 없는 것에서 볼 수 있는 것으로 바꾸는 첫 번째 단계이다."라고 말했다. 물론 모든 사람이 다른 목적, 욕망, 목표를 가지고 있다. 누군가는 좋은 직업을 구하기 위하여, 결혼하기 위하여 혹은 세계여행을 하기 위하여와 같은 장기 목표를 가진다. 다른 이들은 시험 만점 받기, 마라톤 완주하기 혹은 새로운 취미를 갖기 같은 단기 목표를 갖는다.

장기이건 단기이건, 목표를 갖는 것은 자신이 진짜 원하는 것이 무엇이든 목표를 향해 행동하게 만든다. 목표가 없다면 성공에 대한 열렬한 열정이 있어도 진행되지 않는다. 첫 번째 해야 하는 것은 자신의 인생에서 중요한 것이 무엇인지 심사숙고하는 것이다. 그리고 그 과정 동안 여러 가지 문제를 극복해야 한다는 사실을 인정해야 한다. 예외는 없다. 약간의 희생은 치러져야 한다.

감당도 안 될 일을 너무 벌이지는 말아라. 그러나 너의 목표를 이룰 수 있는 전략 아래 목표를 높게 잡아라. 구체적이고, 측정할 수 있고, 도달 가능하고, 현실적이며 시간에 국한되는 걸 의미하는 SMART한 방법이 하나의 전략이다. 구체적인 것은 너의 목표를 명백하게 만들고 목표 측정은 진척을 확실하게 해준다. 너의 목표를 도달 가능하게 만듦으로써, 너는 그저 꿈꾸는 것보다 어떻게 목표를 실제로 달성할 수 있는지 알아낼 수 있다. 덧붙여, 시간을 낭비하지 않기 위해 반드시 목표는 적절한 것이어야 한다. 결국에는 시간이 금이다. 따라서 당신이 제한 시간 안에 목표가 달성 가능하도록 확실히 하여 당신이 적정한 목표 마감일 이내에 달성해야 하는 긴박감을 가질 수 있게 하라.

Unit 01. Setting Goals

Key Vocabulary and Phrases

1. Aim
2. Acing a test
3. Ardent
4. Desire
5. Goal
6. Invisible
7. Visible
8. Ponder
9. Sacrifice
10. Strategy
11. Unambiguous
12. Sense of urgency
13. Obstacle
14. Attainable

Idioms and Expressions

1. There are no ifs and buts about it
2. Aim for the sky
3. Don't bite off more than you can chew
4. Time is money

Explore Further

On YouTube listen to the TED talk by Tony Robbins

Why We Do What We Do

Fill in the blanks with the appropriate word.

1. In business, having the right ____________ is the key to success.

2. If you want to achieve great things, you should set ______________.

3. Someone who is an _________ fan always cheers for the team, even when the team is having a bad season.

4. Korean mothers are known to _____________ their jobs to raise the family.

5. Any goal is ________________ if you set your mind to it.

Match the word with the one that shows its opposite meaning

1. Ponder	a) Dispassionate
2. Ardent	b) Despise
3. Unambiguous	c) Overlook
4. Obstacle	d) Incentive
5. Desire	e) Lucid

Unit 01. Setting Goals

Conversation Starters

1. What is the difference between a goal and a dream?
   Do they mean the same thing?
2. What short-term goals do you have?
3. What are your long-term goals?
4. When you were a child, what dreams did you have about your future?
5. What is your biggest goal in life?
6. Can you discuss some goals that you are proud to have achieved?
7. What are your educational goals, career goals, and spiritual goals?
8. Have you given up on any goals in the past? Do you have any unrealistic goals?
9. If you can achieve or have anything in the world, what would it be?
10. Why is goal setting so important to our lives?

Assignment

Write a sentence using each of the key vocabulary word and idiom given above.

Vocabulary

1.
2.
3.
4.
5.
6.
7.
8.
9.
10.
11.
12.
13.
14.

Idioms

1.
2.
3.

Unit 01. Setting Goals

Presentation Idea

Give a presentation on your short-term and long-term goals and on your plans to attain them.

Definition of Key Words

- **Aim** v. — to direct a course; to point a weapon at an object; *Don't aim the pistol at me!*
- **Aim** n. — a goal or purpose; the ability to hit a target; *The book has two basic aims.*
  Synonyms : goal, ambition, aspiration, purpose, target
  Origin : Middle English, from Anglo-French, first known use in the 14th century
- **Ardent** adj. — characterized by warm feeling; expressed in zealous support or activity;
  She made ardent declarations of love to the man she someday hoped to marry.
  Synonyms : fervent, blazing, burning, fiery, passionate
  Origin : Middle English, from Middle French, first known use in the 15th century
- **Desire** v. — to want or wish for something; to want to have sex with someone;
  He desired her approval more than anything.
- **Desire** n. — the feeling of wanting something; a strong wish;
  Desire is a common theme in music and literature.
  Synonyms : appetite, craving, hankering, itch, lust
  Origin : Middle English, from Anglo-French, first known use in the 13th century
- **Goal** n. — something that you are trying to do or achieve; the end toward which effort is directed; an area or object into which a ball or puck must be hit to score points in various games;
  Her primary goal is to get a college degree.
  Synonyms : aim, ambition, intention, objective, target
  Origin : Middle English, first known use in 1531
- **Invisible** adj. — incapable by nature of being seen; inaccessible to view; not reflected in statistics;
  Homelessness is no longer an invisible problem for this city.
  Synonyms : discreet, inconspicuous, unobtrusive, unnoticeable
  Origin : Middle English, from Anglo-French, first known use in the 14th century

- **Visible** adj. able to be seen, easily seen or understood, capable of being discovered or perceived; *The ship was barely visible.*
  Synonyms : apparent, observable, seeable, visual
  Origin : Middle English, from Middle French or Latin, first known use in the 14th century

- **Ponder** v. to weigh in the mind; to think about deeply; *The team pondered their chances of success.*
  Synonyms : chew over, contemplate, deliberate, meditate, mull over
  Origin : Middle English, from Middle French, first known use in the 14th century

- **Sacrifice** n. the act of giving up something that you want to keep especially in order to get something else; an act of killing a person or animal in a religious ceremony; a person or animal that is killed in a sacrifice; *The war required everyone to make sacrifices.*

- **Sacrifice** v. to give up especially in order to get or do something else or to help someone; to kill in a religious ceremony as an offering to please a god
  Synonyms : immolation, offering, victim
  Origin : Middle English, from Anglo-French, first known use in the 13th century

- **Strategy** n. a careful plan or method for achieving a particular goal usually over a long period of time; the skill of making or carrying out plans to achieve a goal; *They are proposing a new strategy for treating the AIDS virus.*
  Synonyms : arrangement, blueprint, master plan, game plan, ground plan
  Origin : Greek, first known use in 1810

- **Unambiguous** adj. clearly expressed or understood; not ambiguous; *She gave a clear, unambiguous answer.*
  Synonyms : apparent, clear-cut, lucid, obvious, unambivalent
  Origin : first known use in 1743

- **Obstacle** n. something that makes it difficult to do something; an object that you have to go around or over; something that blocks your path; *English is an obstacle that I will have to overcome to land my dream job.*
  Synonyms : deterrent, drag, handicap, hurdle, impediment
  Origin : Middle English, from Anglo-French, first known use in the 14th century

- **Attain** v. to accomplish or achieve something; to succeed in getting or doing something; to grow or increase in a particular amount, size, etc.; *The car can attain a top speed of 200 mph.*
  Origin : Middle English, from Anglo-French, first known use in the 14th century

pp. 18~22 한국어 해설

목표설정

주요 단어 및 구절

1. 목표
2. 시험 만점 받기
3. 열렬한
4. 열정 / 욕망
5. 목표
6. 눈에 보이지 않는
7. 눈에 보이는 / 가시적인
8. 심사숙고 하다
9. 희생
10. 전략
11. 명백한
12. 절박감
13. 장애물
14. 달성할 수 있는

숙어 및 표현

1. 예외가 없다
2. 목표를 높게 갖다
3. 감당도 안 될 일을 벌이지 말아라
4. 시간이 돈이다

빈칸 채우기

1. strategy
2. goals
3. ardent
4. sacrifice
5. attainable

반대의 의미 단어 찾기

1. c
2. a
3. e
4. d
5. b

대화 질문

1. 목표를 가지는 것과 꿈을 가지는 것은 무엇이 다른가?
   똑같은 뜻인가?
2. 당신의 단기목표들은 무엇인가?
3. 당신의 장기목표들은 무엇인가?
4. 당신이 어렸을 때 미래에 대한 어떤 꿈들을 가지고 있었는가?
5. 인생에 제일 큰 목표는 무엇인가?
6. 당신이 달성한 자랑스러운 목표들에 대해 말해 볼 수 있는가?
7. 당신의 교육적인 목표, 직업 목표, 정신적인 목표는 무엇인가?
8. 당신은 과거에 목표를 포기한 적이 있는가?
   비현실적인 목표가 있는가?
9. 만약 세상에 있는 모든 것을 달성하거나 가질 수 있다면
   그것은 무엇일까?
10. 우리의 삶에 목표설정이 중요한 이유는 무엇인가?

과제

위에 주어진 단어와 숙어를 가지고 문장을 만드시오.

발표 아이디어

너의 단기목표와 장기목표 그리고 이루기 위한 계획을 발표하시오.

Unit 02

Thriving in the Job Market

The life of a Korean millennial is tough. The Organization for Economic Co-operation and Development (OECD) lists South Korea as having one of the highest youth unemployment rates among all advanced countries. However, when the going gets tough, the tough gets going. Firms are always on the lookout for that diamond in the rough, and you can make it much easier for them to find you by having an arsenal of skills that will help you thrive in the job market.

Earlier, half of it was just showing up, but now employers are accustomed to having an abundance of choices in a job market that favors employers. Some applicants with advanced degrees even look for entry-level positions for which they are overqualified. A few tangible and intangible skills are needed to really standout and thrive.

Google, for example, hires applicants with both a big ego and a small ego. Having a big ego is a sign of self-confidence, which is needed because the first step to accomplishing something big is to actually believe in it. Google also needs those with a small ego, who can be humble enough to accept criticism when they are wrong and move on. Accepting criticism does not mean that you embrace your flaws but that you find ways for continuous self-development. To get hired at Google, you not only need a thick skin to accept criticism but also the confidence to believe in your success.

Other helpful skills needed to thrive are having a positive attitude and tech-savvy skills and being fluent in at least one other foreign language. Positivity is infectious. Everyone including your boss enjoys being around an optimistic person. Besides, being proficient in Microsoft Office, Adobe Photoshop, or coding skills such as Java will give you an edge over your peers. Finally, customers can be next door or anywhere around the world, and having the right language skills can open up the doors for you to do business.

- Key Vocabulary
- Idioms and Expressions

해석

취업전선에서 성공하기

한국의 천년 세대들의 삶은 가혹하다. OECD는 한국을 선진국 중에 청년실업률이 제일 높은 나라로 선정했다. 그러나 상황이 힘들어지면 강한 사람들은 더 강해진다. 회사들은 항상 진흙 속의 다이아몬드를 찾고 있기에 당신이 기량과 가능성을 많이 가지고 있다면 취업전선에서 살아남기가 훨씬 쉬울 것이다.

예전에는 절반만이 나타났지만 현재 고용인들은 취업시장에서 원하는 인재를 선발하는 것에 대한 수많은 선택권을 갖는데 익숙하다. 고급 학위를 가진 몇몇 지원자들도 심지어 자신들로서는 필요 이상의 자격을 갖추게 된 꼴인 신입직을 원한다. 몇 개의 무형 유형 기술들이 눈에 띄고 살아남기 위해 필요하다.

예를 들어 구글은 자신감이 넘치는 사람과 자신감이 적은 지원자들을 다 고용한다. 넘치는 자신감은 자신감의 상징이다. 왜냐하면 어떤 큰 것을 성취하는 것의 첫 번째 단계는 진실로 믿는 것이기 때문이다. 구글은 그들이 잘못할 때 충분히 비판을 받아들이고 앞으로 나아갈 수 있는 자존심을 줄일 수 있는 지원자 또한 필요하다. 비판을 받아들이는 것은 자신의 결함을 포용하는 것이 아니라 지속적인 자기 개발을 할 방법을 찾는 것이다. 구글에서 일하려면 비판을 수용하는 철면피가 필요한 것뿐만 아니라 자신의 성공에 대한 믿음도 필요하다.

살아남기 위해 도움되는 다른 방법은 긍정적인 태도, 기계에 대한 뛰어난 지식, 최소 한 가지 외국어에 유창한 것이다. 적극성은 전염된다. 상사를 포함한 모든 사람들이 낙천적인 사람들과 있기를 좋아한다. 게다가 MS Office, 어도비 포토샵 혹은 자바 같은 코딩기술에 능숙하면 동료들보다 당신이 우세하도록 해준다. 마지막으로, 고객들은 옆집에 또한 도처에 있을 수 있기에 올바른 언어능력은 당신에게 사업을 보다 더 잘할 수 있는 기회를 열어 줄 수도 있다.

Unit 02. Thriving in the Job Market

Key Vocabulary and Phrases

1. Millennials
2. OECD
3. Abundance
4. Accustomed
5. Accomplish
6. Arsenal
7. Thrive
8. To standout
9. Ego
10. Confidence
11. Criticism
12. Embrace
13. Infectious
14. Optimistic
15. Savvy
16. Fluent
17. An edge
18. Open up the doors...
19. Tangible and intangible
20. Proficient

Idioms and Expressions

1. When the going gets tough, the tough gets going
2. Diamond in the rough
3. Half of it is just showing up
4. Having a thick skin

Explore Further

On YouTube listen to the TED talk by Scott Hess

Millenials - Who They Are & Why We Hate Them

Unit 02. Thriving in the Job Market

Fill in the blanks with the appropriate word

1. Ebola is a highly __________ disease so you should be careful where you travel.

2. She is ______________ in three languages.

3. Despite his large ______________, he really was not that good of a singer.

4. Some soccer players who are short seem to be more _____________ in dribbling the ball.

5. You should ____________ your flaws, since everyone has them.

Match the word with the one showing its opposite meaning

1. Confidence	**a)** Wither
2. Abundance	**b)** Dearth
3. Thrive	**c)** Sensitive
4. Thick skin	**d)** Pessimistic
5. Optimistic	**e)** Insecurity

Conversation Questions

1. How is the job market in your city or region? Can you describe it?
2. What are the most popular companies to work for in your area?
3. What kind of skills are employers seeking these days?
4. Have you recently worked on improving any of your skills?
5. Among your friends, who has the best job? What skills does he/she possess?
6. Are you good at receiving criticism? What kind of criticism have you received in the past? Did you improve?
7. In what areas do you feel confident? How can you improve your confidence?
8. What are your strong points and weak points? How can you improve your weak points?
9. What job would you most like to do and why?

Assignment

Write a sentence using each of the key vocabulary word and idiom given above.

Unit 02. Thriving in the Job Market

Vocabulary

1.

2.

3.

4.

5.

6.

7.

8.

9.

10.

11.

12.

13.

14.

15.

16.

17.

18.

19.

20.

21.

Idioms

1.

2.

3.

Definition of Key Words

- **Millennial** adj. — of or relating to a millennium

- **Millennial** n. — a person born in the 1980s or 1990s – usually plural;
  Millennials feel different about many social issues as compared to the older generations.
  Origin: first known use in 1991

- **Abundance** n. — a large amount of something; affluence, wealth; ***This plant has an abundance of flowers.***
  Synonyms: boatload, heap, profusion, plentitude, much
  Origin: first known use in the 14th century

- **Accustomed** adj. — familiar with something so that it seems normal or usual; usual or regular;
  He was accustomed to winning on the basketball court.
  Synonyms: given, habituated, used, wont
  Origin: first known use in the 15th century

- **Accomplishment** n. — something done or achieved successfully; the successful completion of something; special skill or ability gained by practice or training;
  Her family is proud of all her academic accomplishments.
  Synonyms: acquirement, attainment, success, triumph
  Origin: first known use in the 15th century

- **Arsenal** n. — a collection of weapons; a place where weapons are made or stored; a group of things or people that are available to be used; ***Doctors have a broad arsenal of medicine to choose from.***
  Synonyms: armory, depot, dump, magazine
  Origin: from Italian, ultimately from Arabic, first known use in 1555

Unit 02. Thriving in the Job Market

- **Thrive** v.

  to grow or develop successfully; to flourish or succeed;
  These plants thrive with little sunlight.
  Synonyms: burgeon, flourish, prosper
  Origin: from Middle English, from Old Norse, first known use in the 13th century

- **Ego** n.

  the opinion that you have about yourself;
  a part of the mind that senses and adapts to the real world;
  He has a huge ego from being a star athlete in college.
  Synonyms: pride, self-esteem, self-regard, self-respect
  Origin: New Latin, first known use in 1789

- **Confidence** n.

  a feeling or belief that you can do something well; a feeling or belief that someone or something has the ability to succeed; the feeling that something will happen;
  The class gave me more confidence to speak English.
  Synonyms: assurance, self-assurance, self-esteem, self-confidence
  Origin: first known use in the 14th century

- **Criticism** n.

  the act of expressing disapproval and of noting the problems or faults of a person or thing; the act of criticizing someone or something;
  a remark that expresses disapproval of someone or something; the activity of making careful judgments about the good and bad qualities of books, movies, etc.;
  I had one minor criticism about her design.
  Synonyms: critique, notice, review
  Origin: first known use in 1607.

- **Embrace** v.

  to hold someone in your arms as a way of expressing love or friendship;
  to accept readily or gladly; to use eagerly;
  Bill Clinton was embraced by people of all races.
  Synonyms: bear-hug, clasp, enfold, grasp, strain
  Origin: Middle English, from Anglo-French, first known use in the 14th century

- **Infectious** adj.

  capable of causing infection; capable of being passed to someone else by germs that enter the body; suffering from a disease that can be spread to other people by germs;
  He has an infectious smile.
  Synonyms: catching, epidemic, contagious, spreading
  Origin: first known use in 1542

- **Optimistic** n. — a feeling or belief that good things will happen in the future; a feeling or belief that what you hope for will happen; *The early sales reports are cause for optimism.*
Synonyms: bullishness, sanguinity
Origin: French, first known use in 1759

- **Savvy** n. — practical understanding or knowledge of something; *She's excellent at English but lacks any savvy in math.*
Synonyms: chops, expertise, know-how, proficiency, skills

- **Savvy** adj. — showing perception, comprehension, or shrewdness especially in practical matters; *She's a very savvy investor.*
Origin: first known use in 1905

- **Fluent** adj. — able to speak a language easily and very well; done in a smooth and easy way; *Alex is a fluent speaker of Chinese, English, and Korean.*
Synonyms: eloquent, articulate, silver-tongued, well-spoken
Origin: first known use in 1585

- **Tangible** adj. — easily seen or recognized; able to be touched or felt; *There is no tangible evidence to support her claim.*
Synonyms: palpable, touchable
Origin: Latin, first known use in 1589

- **Proficient** adj. — good at doing something; *She is proficient in two foreign languages.*
Synonyms: adept, consummate, educated, masterful, versed
Origin: Latin, first known use in 1590

pp. 27~29 한국어 해설

취업전선에서 성공하기

주요단어 및 구절

1. 천 년
2. 경제협력개발기구
3. 풍부
4. 익숙한
5. 업적을 이루다 / 성취하다
6. 비축 / 무기
7. 성공하다
8. 눈에 띄다
9. 자부심
10. 자신감
11. 비판
12. 받아들이다
13. 전염되는
14. 낙천적인 / 낙관적인
15. 지식
16. 능숙한 / 유창한
17. 우세함 / 유리함
18. 기회를 주다
19. 유형 무형의
20. 철면피
21. 능숙한

숙어 및 표현

1. 상황이 힘들어지면 강인한 사람들은 더 강해진다
2. 진흙 속의 다이아몬드
3. 절반만이 나타나다
4. 철면피를 가지다 – 뻔뻔하다

빈칸 채우기

1. Infectious
2. Fluent
3. Ego
4. Savvy
5. Embrace

반대의 의미 단어 찾기

1. e
2. b
3. A
4. c
5. d

대화 질문

1. 당신의 도시나 지역의 취업시장은 어떤가? 설명할 수 있는가?
2. 당신의 지역에서 일하기 좋은 가장 인기 있는 회사들은 무엇인가?
3. 요즘 고용인들이 원하는 기술들은 무엇인가?
4. 요즘 너의 기술을 개발하기 위해 노력한 적이 있는가?
5. 너의 친구들 중, 누가 가장 좋은 직업을 가지고 있는가?
   그들은 무슨 기술을 가지고 있는가?
6. 너는 비판을 잘 받아 낼 수 있는가? 과거에 어떤 비판을 받았었나?
   넌 향상되었는가?
7. 어떤 분야에 자신감이 있는가? 자신감을 어떻게 향상시켰는가?
8. 너의 강점과 약점은 무엇인가? 약점은 어떻게 고칠 수 있는가?
9. 어떤 일을 가장 하고 싶은가? 이유는?

과제

위에 주어진 단어와 숙어를 가지고 문장을 만드시오.

Unit 03

Choosing Jobs

Have passion for the job you choose. You do not want to burn out. However, there may be a trade-off between doing what you love and in doing what pays. You always cannot have the best of both worlds. An example is the starving artist who just gets by but is able to focus on his/her artwork. Regardless, if you have the passion for something, go for it. Nonetheless, to be ahead of the curve, at least know the hot jobs of the future.

Where you decide to live may influence what job you choose. In the U.S., aspiring fashion designers flock to New York and hopeful actors take off for California. If you are interested in being an oil engineer, Texas is suitable and if you like tourism, convention, and gambling, perhaps Nevada will do.

Another factor in choosing a job is to consider the type of industry. For instance, the clock is ticking on traditional newspaper firms because of on-line media. If you consider apparel manufacturing, I bet most of your clothes are made overseas. Choosing a job in a rapidly declining industry can lead you to miss the boat on industry growth so keep an eye on the future. After all, a rising tide lifts all boats. For example, 20 years ago, Yoga was unheard of in the U.S. but now it is ubiquitous in every major city. If you were in the yoga business at the vanguard of its rise, there is no telling how successful you would be now.

Another consideration in developed countries is the transformation to a knowledge-based economy. Globalization has led everyone to be wired and connected, resulting in greater exchanges of ideas and technology. Advanced countries have shifted their economy to these fields because there is more added value and money to be earned. For instance, South Korea's economy is heavy on electronic devices such as smart phones based on technological know-how because those products are more profitable than dealings in agricultural products.

To succeed in a knowledge-based economy, education holds the key. STEM is an acronym referring to science, technology, engineering, and mathematics. Many industry titans such as Bill Gates have called for the U.S. to support STEM education because firms need workers with the knowledge to develop the services and products of the future. Students from STEM fields are more likely to enter a field with higher demand.

The monkey wrench for international students is that on top of their regular STEM education, they are expected to speak excellent English because it has become the lingua franca of today. For those entering into the labor market, there are many things to worry about.

- Key Vocabulary
- Idioms and Expressions

해석

직업 선택하기

당신이 선택한 직업에 열정을 가져라. 당신은 에너지를 소진하기를 원하진 않는다. 그러나 당신이 좋아하는 일과 돈을 버는 일에는 균형이 있을 수 있다. 양쪽 세계를 다 만족시킬 수는 없다. 밥도 잘 못 먹을 정도로 그럭저럭 지내지만 자기 예술작업에 집중할 수 있는 예술가가 한 예이다. 당신이 무언가에 열정이 있다면 개의치 말고 그 일을 해라. 그렇더라도, 시대에 앞서서 최소한 미래 유망직종은 알아두도록 해라.

당신이 살기로 결정한 장소는 직업선택에 영향을 미친다. 미국에서는 야심에 찬 패션디자이너들이 뉴욕으로 모여들고 희망에 찬 배우들은 캘리포니아로 떠나간다. 당신이 석유공학자가 되는 것에 관심이 있다면 텍사스가 알맞고, 만약 관광업, 컨벤션 그리고 도박이 좋다면 아마 네바다가 좋을 것이다.

직업을 정하는데 다른 요소는 산업의 종류를 고려하는 것이다. 예를 들어 온라인 미디어 때문에 전통적인 신문 회사들이 문을 닫는 시간이 다가오고 있다. 만약 의류 제조업을 고려해 본다면, 나는 너의 대부분의 옷들이 해외에서 만들어졌다고 본다. 급격히 감소하는 산업의 직업을 고르는 것은 너를 산업 성장에서의 기회를 놓치게 만들 수 있다. 따라서 미래를 항상 지켜봐라. 결국 밀물은 모든 배를 뜨게 만든다. 예를 들면 20년 전에, 요가는 미국에서 전례가 없었다. 그러나 지금 요가는 대도시 어디에나 있다. 떠오르는 요가 산업의 선두에 당신이 있었다면, 당신이 지금 얼마나 성공했을지는 알 수 없다.

선진국에서의 다른 고려사항은 지식 기반 경제로의 변화이다. 세계화는 모두를 연결되고 결합하게 만들어서 더 나은 아이디어와 기술의 교환을 야기했다. 더 많은 부가가치와 더 많은 돈을 벌 수 있기 때문에 선진국들은 이런 분야로 경제를 옮겼다. 예를 들어, 남한의 경제는 기술적 노하우에 근거한 스마트 폰 같은 전자기기에 상당히 치중해 있다. 왜냐하면 이런 제품들이 농산품을 다루는 것보다 더 수익성이 있기 때문이다.

지식 기반 사회에서 성공하기 위해 교육이 열쇠를 쥐고 있다. STEM은 과학, 기술, 공학 그리고 수학의 앞 글자를 따온 것이다. 빌 게이츠 같은 많은 산업의 거부들은 회사들이 미래에 서비스와 제품을 발전시키기 위하여 지식이 있는 직원이 필요하기 때문에 STEM교육을 지원해 주길 미국에게 요청했다. STEM분야의 학생들은 수요가 많은 그 분야에 좀 더 쉽게 들어갈 수 있다.

국제 학생들의 장애물은 정규 STEM교육 뿐만이 아니라 영어가 오늘날 국제언어가 된 이후로 그들은 영어에 능통하기를 기대된다는 것이다. 취업 시장에 들어가는 사람들은 많은 걱정거리가 있다.

Unit 03. Choosing Jobs

Key Vocabulary and Phrases

1. Passion
2. Focus
3. Aspiring
4. Media
5. Industry
6. Overseas
7. Rapidly
8. Ubiquitous
9. Vanguard
10. Globalization
11. Wired
12. Starving Artist
13. Just get by
14. Go for it
15. Hot job
16. Flock
17. Labor market
18. Titan

Idioms and Expressions

1. Burn out
2. Trade-off
3. Ahead of the curve
4. Miss the boat
5. Monkey wrench
6. The clock is ticking
7. Hold the key
8. Have the best of both worlds
9. A rising tide lifts all boats

Fill in the blanks with the appropriate word

1. ____________ is the key ingredient to succeed and continue in any endeavor.

2. The ICT ____________ is responsible for most of the economy's new growth.

3. Many factory jobs have been ________________ to China.

4. For some reason, throwing up the peace sign while taking pictures is __________ in Korea.

5. Even though he drove a nice car, in actuality, he was living with his mom and ______________.

Match the word with the one that shows its opposite meaning

1. Aspiring	**a)** Regional
2. Overseas	**b)** Followers
3. Ubiquitous	**c)** Solo
4. Vanguard	**d)** Scarce
5. Flock	**e)** Descend

Explore Further

On YouTube listen to the TED talk by Scott Dinsmore

How to Find and Do Work You Love

Unit 03. Choosing Jobs

Conversation Questions

1. What are the hot industries in your country?
2. What industries are rapidly declining in your country?
3. Are you more of a science and engineering person or more of a humanities person?
4. What is your dream job and why?
5. How did you get your last job? Did personal relationships help you?
6. How important are school, family, and regional relationships in Korea to get a job? Please provide examples from your own experience.
7. Among the people you know, who has the best job? Why do you consider it the best job?
8. Would you like to work abroad? If so, in which country and why?
9. What jobs are likely to be outsourced in the future?
10. What are the main industries in your region and city?

Assignment

Write a sentence using each of the key vocabulary word and idiom given above.

Vocabulary

1. ____________________

2. ____________________

3. ____________________

4. ____________________

5. ____________________

6.

7.

8.

9.

10.

11.

12.

13.

14.

15.

16.

17.

18.

Idioms

1.

2.

3.

4.

5.

6.

7. ____________________

8. ____________________

9. ____________________

Definition of Key Words

- **Aspire** v. — to want to have or achieve something such as a particular career or level of success;
  I hope you aspire to help others after you become successful.
  Synonyms: aim, allow, intend, calculate, design, plan
  Origin: Middle English, from Middle French, first known use in the 14th century

- **Media** n. — a medium of cultivation, conveyance, or expression; members of the mass media;
  A lot of liberals in America dislike Fox media.
  Origin: first known use in 1923

- **Rapid** adj. — happening in a short amount of time; having a fast rate; moving quickly;
  There's been rapid growth in the number of new businesses in the town.
  Synonyms: breakneck, breathless, hasty, speedy, swift
  Origin: first known use in 1634

- **Ubiquitous** adj. — seeming to be seen everywhere; *The company's advertisements are ubiquitous.*
  Synonyms: commonplace, everyday, familiar, garden-variety, ordinary
  Origin: first known use in 1830

- **Vanguard** n. — the group of people who are the leaders of an action or movement in society, politics, art, etc.;
  Martin Luther king was at the vanguard of the Civil Rights Movement.
  Synonyms: cutting edge, van, avant-garde
  Origin: Middle English, from Anglo-French, first known use in the 15th century

- **Wired** adj. — very excited or full of nervous energy; connected to the Internet;
  No more caffeine for me, I'm pretty wired.
  Origin: first known use in the 15th century

- **Flock** n. — a group of animals like birds and sheep assembled or herded together;
  a group under the guidance of a leader, especially a church congregation;
  a large number of tourist

- **Flock** v. — to gather or move in a flock; *They flocked to the beach.*
  Origin: Middle English, from Old English, first known use in the 13th century.

- **Titan** n. — one of a family of giants in Greek mythology;
  an extremely large and powerful person, company, etc.
  John D. Rockefeller was a famous oil titan of the early 20th century.
  Synonyms: behemoth, blockbuster, colossus, elephant, giant, whopper
  Origin: Greek, first known use in 1741

pp. 38~40 한국어 해설

직업 선택하기

주요단어 및 구절

1. 열정
2. 집중하다, 초점을 맞추다
3. 떠오르는, 야심에 찬
4. 미디어, 대중매체
5. 산업
6. 해외의
7. 빨리, 급격히
8. 어디에나 있는, 아주 흔한
9. 선두, 선봉
10. 세계화
11. 연결된
12. 예술을 위해 돈을 포기한 예술가
13. 그럭저럭 지내다
14. 시도하다
15. 유망직종
16. 모이다
17. 노동시장
18. 거물, 거인

숙어 및 표현

1. 에너지를 소진하다
2. 균형을 유지하다, 균형
3. 시대에 앞서서, 유행에 앞서서
4. 기회를 놓치다
5. 장애물
6. 시간이 흘러가다, 시간이 촉박하다
7. 열쇠를 쥐고 있다
8. 양 측면을 다 만족시키다
9. 밀물은 모든 배를 뜨게 만든다

빈칸 채우기

1. Passion
2. Industry
3. Outsourced
4. Ubiquitous
5. Just getting by

반대의 의미 단어 찾기

1. e
2. a
3. d
4. b
5. c

대화질문

1. 당신의 나라에서 유망산업은 무엇인가?
2. 당신의 나라에서 급격히 쇠퇴하고 있는 산업은 무엇인가?
3. 당신은 이공계에 가까운 사람인가 아니면 인문계에 가까운 사람인가?
4. 당신이 꿈꾸는 직업은 무엇인가? 이유는?
5. 당신은 전 직장을 어떻게 구했는가? 인간관계가 도움이 되었는가?
6. 학교, 가족 그리고 지역 관계가 한국에서 직장을 구하는데 얼마나 중요한가? 자신이 한 경험을 예로 들어보라.
7. 당신이 아는 사람들 중에 누가 가장 좋은 직업을 갖고 있나? 왜 그 직업이 최고라고 생각하는가?
8. 당신은 해외에서 일하고 싶은가? 만약 그렇다면 어떤 나라를 원하고 왜 원하는가?
9. 미래에 어떤 직업들이 위탁 될 것인가?
10. 당신의 지역과 도시의 주요 산업은 무엇인가?

과제

위에 주어진 단어와 숙어를 가지고 문장을 만드시오.

Unit 04

Best Places to Work

Korean graduates are obsessed with landing a great job, which is understandable considering that some firms are really great places to work. They offer not only the standard benefits such as daycare, maternity leave, and insurance but also fringe benefits such as enticing stock options, free gourmet food, and a fun work environment. Following are some of the firms voted as one of the best places to work.

Starbucks: Starbucks announced that it would pay for thousands of its employees to complete their bachelor's degree. It hopes to pay employee's tuition charges at select universities or to offer some sort of reimbursement. Some critics have looked at the fine print however and claim that many of its employees are ineligible for the program and that Starbucks is just attempting a publicity stunt to increase brand image.

Amazon: The on-line retailer Amazon is another popular firm. Amazon actually pays new employees $5000 to quit their jobs. There really is no catch; they just figure that the company is better off without having employees who only stick around for the next paycheck. The CEO Jeff Bezos explained "an employee staying somewhere they don't want to be isn't healthy for the employee or the company." Even though Amazon offers money for unmotivated employees to quit, 97% of employees decline and stay at the company.

Google: The perennial best place to work according to *Fortune* magazine's annual survey is Google. They offer perks such as gourmet food, on-site laundry, and nap rooms with futuristic sleeping chairs. Google really pulls it off by using social scientists to run experiments on how they can make employees happy. For example, they studied whether employees would be happier with a year-end bonus or an incremental bump in salary. As workers wanted extra pay in salary, everyone got a 10% salary increase.

We spend a large portion of our lives at our work place. Workers even break their backs so the company can prosper. It is too bad that many firms are out of touch with the needs of workers. A happy worker can be more productive and effective. Hopefully in the future, more companies can get with the program and realize that what is good for the worker is also good for the firm.

• Key Vocabulary
• Idioms and Expressions

해석

일하기 가장 좋은 직장

한국의 졸업생들은 좋은 직업을 갖는 것에 사로잡혀 있다. 어떤 회사들은 일하기 정말 좋다는 걸 고려할 때 그것은 이해할 만하다. 좋은 직장들은 탁아시설, 출산휴가 그리고 보험 같은 보통의 혜택을 제공하는 것뿐만 아니라 부가혜택인 매혹적인 스톡옵션, 무료 고급식품 그리고 재미있는 근무환경도 제공한다. 아래 보기들은 가장 일하기 좋은 곳으로 뽑힌 회사들이다.

스타벅스 : 스타벅스는 수천 달러를 직원들의 학사학위 취득을 위해 지불하겠다고 밝혔다. 스타벅스는 엄선한 대학들의 직원들의 수업료 혹은 상환 같은 것을 지불하길 희망한다. 세세한 항목을 본 몇몇 비평가들은 많은 직원들이 그 프로그램에 부적격하며 스타벅스가 단지 브랜드 이미지를 높이기 위해 떠들썩한 선전을 시도한다고 주장했다.

아마존 : 온라인 소매상인 아마존은 다른 인기 있는 회사이다. 실제로 아마존은 일을 그만두는 신입직원에게 5,000달러를 준다. 여기엔 대단한 속셈이 있는 것은 아니다. 단지 회사는 다음 달 월급만을 기다리며 머무르는 직원들을 데리고 있는 것보다는 이게 더 낫다고 판단한 것이다. CEO인 제프 베조스는 "그들이 원하지 않는 곳에 머무르는 직원들은 그 직원을 위해서나 회사를 위해서나 좋지 않다."라고 설명했다. 비록 아마존이 동기가 없는 직원들에게 그만두라고 돈을 지급하는데도 불구하고, 97%의 직원들이 이를 거절하고 회사에 남았다.

구글 : 〈포춘〉지의 연례 조사에 따르면 일하기 좋은 최고의 직장으로 해마다 구글이 뽑힌다고 밝혀졌다. 그들은 고급 식료품, 구내(회사내) 세탁실 그리고 미래적인 수면 의자가 있는 낮잠 자는 방 같은 비금전적 혜택을 제공한다. 구글은 어떻게 하면 그들이 직원들을 행복하게 할 수 있는지의 실험을 위해 사회학자들을 정말 잘 이용한다. 예를 들어 2,000달러의 연말 보너스와 기본급 1,000달러 인상 중 무엇을 더 직원들이 좋아하는지 연구했다. 직원들이 급료 인상을 원하기 때문에, 모든 직원의 급료가 10% 인상되었다.

우리는 우리 삶의 큰 부분을 직장에서 보내고 있다. 노동자들은 회사가 번영하기 위하여 뼈빠지게 일한다. 많은 기업들이 노동자들이 원하는 것과 멀어지는 것은 애석하다. 행복한 노동자는 더 생산적이고 효율적일 수 있다. 바라건대 미래에는, 더 많은 회사들이 태도를 바꾸어 노동자들에게 좋은 것이 회사에게도 좋은 것임을 깨달을 수 있으면 한다.

Unit 04. Best Places to Work

Key Vocabulary and Phrases

1. Obsessed
2. Standard
3. Maternity leave
4. Fringe benefits
5. Enticing
6. Reimbursement
7. Critic
8. Ineligible
9. Publicity
10. Perennial
11. Bump
12. Fine print
13. Figure
14. On-site
15. Too bad
16. Getting with the program

Idioms and Expressions

1. The catch is / What's the catch?
2. Stick around
3. Pull it off
4. Break your back
5. Out of touch

Fill in the blanks with the appropriate word

1. Koreans are ____________ with learning English.

2. Starbucks has some __________ benefits to attract employees.

3. Lawyers always advise clients to read the _____________ before signing the contract.

4. In the U.S. getting off work by 6 pm is usually _______________.

5. The saying goes that any ___________ is good publicity.

Match the word with the one that shows its opposite meaning

1. Critics	**a)** Repel
2. Reimburse	**b)** Rare
3. Entice	**c)** Compliment
4. Standard	**d)** Disenchanted
5. Obsessed	**e)** Deprive

Explore Further

On YouTube listen to the TED talk by Dan Pink

The Puzzle of Motivation

Unit 04. Best Places to Work

Conversation Questions

1. What job perks are most important to you?
2. What work environment allows you to be most productive?
3. What is more important to you at your job, money or atmosphere?
4. Describe the hallmarks of the best places to work.
5. What are the best firms to work for in your city and why?
6. How can firms increase worker morale and productivity?
7. How do managers affect the work environment?
   Describe your ideal manager.
8. Explain the differences between working for a Korean company and an international company.
9. How does Google attract so much attention as being one of the best places to work every year?
10. Which is your favorite work place and why?
11. Who are your favorite people to work with and why?

Assignment

Write a sentence using each of the key vocabulary word and idiom given above.

Vocabulary

1. ____________________

2. ____________________

3. ____________________

4.

5.

6.

7.

8.

9.

10.

11.

12.

13.

14.

15.

16.

Idioms

1.

2.

3.

4.

5.

Class Idea

In groups, conduct research on some of the best local firms to work for. Focus on hidden champions or on otherwise very good but unnoticed firms that are great places to work.

Unit 04. Best Places to Work

Definition of Key Words

- **Obsess** v.

  to be the only person or thing that someone thinks or talks about;
  to think and talk about someone or something too much;
  The war obsesses him — he talks about nothing else.
  Origin: Latin, first known use in 1531

- **Standard** n.

  a level of quality, achievement, etc. that is considered acceptable or desirable;
  By modern standards, the house is just too small.
  Synonyms: bar, barometer, benchmark, criterion, gold standard
  Origin: Middle English, from Anglo-French, first known use in the 12th century

- **Entice** v.

  to attract someone especially by offering or showing something that is appealing, interesting, etc.;
  I was enticed to the new job because of the opportunity to often travel.
  Synonyms: allure, bait, lure, lead on, seduce, solicit, tempt
  Origin: Middle English, from Anglo-French, first known use in the 14th century

- **Reimburse** v.

  to pay someone an amount of money equal to an amount that person has spent;
  Save your receipts so we can reimburse you for your traveling expenses.
  Synonyms: refund, repay
  Origin: first known use in 1611

- **Critic** n.

  one who expresses a reasoned opinion on any matter especially involving a judgment of its value, truth, righteousness, beauty, or technique; one given to harsh or captious judgment;
  He is a critic of medieval art.
  Origin: Latin, from Greek, first known use in 1588

- **Ineligible** adj.

  not allowed to do or be something; not eligible; *They are ineligible for a loan.*
  Origin: French, first known use in 1770

- **Publicity** n.

  something that attracts the attention of the public;
  attention that is given to someone or something by newspapers, magazines, news, etc.;
  The film has gotten some good publicity.
  Synonyms: ballyhoo, hype, puffery
  Origin: first known use in 1788

- **Perennial** adj.

  existing in the same way for a long time; happening again and again;
  Lack of food is a perennial problem for some people around the world.

pp. 48~51 한국어 해설

일하기 가장 좋은 직장

주요단어 및 구절

1. 사로잡히다, 집착하다
2. 보통의, 표준의
3. 출산휴가
4. 부가혜택
5. 매혹적인, 매력적인
6. 상환
7. 비평가, 비판가
8. 부적격의
9. 선전, 광고
10. 영원한
11. 튀어나온, 오르다, 격상
12. 세세한 항목
13. 판단하다
14. 현장의
15. 애석한
16. 태도를 바꾸어 할 일을 하기[는]

숙어 및 표현

1. 속셈은……/ 무슨 속셈이냐?
2. 머무르다
3. 해내다
4. 뼈빠지게 일하다
5. 멀어져서

빈칸 채우기

1. Obsessed
2. Enticing
3. Fine print
4. Standard
5. Publicity

반대의 의미 단어 찾기

1. c
2. e
3. a
4. b
5. d

질문 대화

1. 당신에게 가장 중요한 직장의 비금전적 혜택은 무엇인가?
2. 당신이 가장 일을 잘할 수 있게 하는 사무실 환경은 무엇인가?
3. 당신의 직업에서 돈과 분위기 중 무엇이 당신에게 더 중요한가?
4. 일하기 가장 좋은 곳의 특징을 설명하라.
5. 당신의 도시에서 일하기 좋은 최고의 회사는 어디인가? 그리고 이유는?
6. 어떻게 회사가 직원들의 사기와 생산성을 증가시킬 수 있는가?
7. 어떻게 관리자가 작업 환경에 영향을 미칠 수 있는가? 당신의 이상적인 관리자를 묘사하라.
8. 한국기업에서 일하는 것과 외국기업에서 일하는 것 사이의 차이점을 설명하라.
9. 구글은 어떻게 일하기 가장 좋은 곳 중 하나로 매년 많은 관심을 끌 수 있는가?
10. 당신이 일하기 가장 좋은 곳은 어디인가? 이유는?
11. 당신이 같이 일하기 좋은 사람들은 누구인가? 이유는?

과제

위에 주어진 단어와 숙어를 가지고 문장을 만드시오.

수업 아이디어

그룹별로 일하기 가장 좋은 지역기업을 조사하라.
숨어 있는 작지만 강한 중소기업 또는 매우 좋으나 알려지지 않은 일하기 좋은 회사들에 초점을 맞추어라.

Unit 05

Resume and Cover Letter

Every job seeker needs a killer resume and cover letter to get the job he/she wants. However if you belive recruiters will scrutinize every word you will be disappointed. To them, sub-par resumes are a dime a dozen. To attract their attention, make sure to revise and peruse your resume for style and grammar.

A study that measured eye movement using a scientific technique called "eye tracking" found that most experienced recruiters spend on average only 6 seconds before deciding on a candidate. With such a short time, irrespective of whether your resume is chronological or functional, highlight pertinent information using a clear visual hierarchy and specify achievements because recruiters look for quantifiable results.

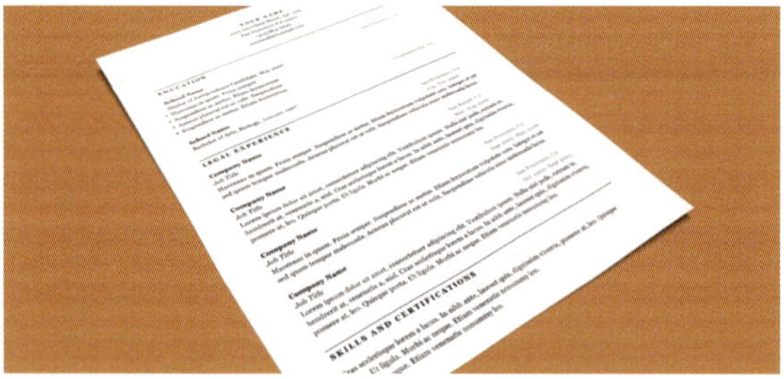

Just remember to never lie or exaggerate on your application. If the recruiters or companies sense you have fudged the truth, you will lose any chance you had to get the job. Besides you never know if they will call your references or other recruiters and this can hurt your reputation. Anyways, it is simply wrong to lie on principle. Although some believe that it is okay as long as the ends justify the means, it is better to be an honest person because our code of conduct touches the lives of those around us.

Now follow advice on the cover letter. Usually a cover letter is sent in tandem with the resume. Before you write it, research the employer and tailor the letter to meet the needs of the company and job description. An exemplary cover letter should reflect your personality. Show your enthusiasm, initiative, and ambition. Proofread your letter and be concise. Getting straight to the point will keep the recruiter focused on you and not on the time he/she is spending reading your letter.

- Key Vocabulary
- Idioms and Expressions

해석

이력서와 자기소개서

모든 구직자는 원하는 직업을 구하기 위하여 죽이는(?) 이력서와 자기소개서가 필요하다. 그러나 모집자들이 글자 하나하나를 세심히 본다고 생각한다면 당신은 실망할 것이다. 그들에겐 보통 이하의 이력서는 흔하고 흔하다. 그들의 관심을 끌기 위해서는 당신의 이력서의 스타일과 문법을 꼭 수정하고 정독해라.

눈길 추적이라 불리는 과학기술을 이용하여 눈의 움직임을 측정한 한 연구에서 숙련된 모집자는 지원자를 결정하기 전에 단지 평균 6초 정도 사용한다는 것을 밝혀냈다. (이력서를 읽는데) 시간이 이처럼 짧기 때문에 이력서가 연대순 배열이든 기능 중심적이든 적절한 정보를 명백하고 보기 쉽게 중요한 순서대로 강조할 뿐만 아니라 업적 또한 구체화하라. 왜냐하면, 모집자들은 수량화할 수 있는 결과를 원하기 때문이다.

너의 지원서에 절대 거짓말이나 과장을 하면 안 된다는 것을 기억하라. 만약 모집자나 회사가 당신이 사실을 날조한 것을 눈치채면 당신은 취직할 수 있는 기회를 잃어버릴 것이다. 게다가 그들이 당신의 추천인이나 다른 모집자들에게 연락하여 당신의 평판을 손상시킬지 아무도 모른다. 어쨌든, 거짓말은 도덕상 옳지 않은 것이다. 비록 다른 사람들은 모로 가도 서울만 가도 된다고 믿지만, 우리의 행동수칙이 주변 사람들과 관련되어 있기 때문에 솔직한 사람이 되는 것이 낫다.

자, 이제는 자기소개서에 대한 충고를 따라라. 보통 자기소개서는 이력서와 함께 동시에 보내진다. 자기소개서를 쓰기 전에 고용인을 연구하고 회사와 직무소개서의 필요에 맞게끔 작성하라. 모범적인 자기소개서는 너의 성격을 반영해야 한다. 당신의 열정, 결단력 그리고 포부를 보여줘라. 이력서를 교정하고 간결화하라. 단도직입적으로 작성하면 모집자가 당신의 지원서를 읽느라 드는 시간에 신경을 쓰는 대신 당신에게 집중할 것이다.

Unit 05. Resume and Cover Letter

Key Vocabulary and Phrases

1. Killer
2. Scrutinize
3. Disappointed
4. Sub-par
5. Revise
6. Peruse
7. Measured
8. Experienced
9. Chronological
10. Functional
11. Pertinent
12. Hierarchy
13. Quantifiable
14. Exaggerate
15. Reference
16. Advice
17. Tandem
18. Tailor
19. Exemplary
20. Enthusiasm
21. Initiative
22. Ambition
23. Wrong to lie on principle
24. Touch the lives of those around us

Idioms and Expressions

1. Getting straight to the point
2. Ends justify the means
3. Fudge the truth
4. Dime a dozen

Fill in the blanks with the appropriate word

1. Ray Allen had a ________ jump shot and holds the record for the most three-pointers in a game.

2. Recruiters are looking for ___________ experiences on the resume.

3. I was _____________ to not receive any present on my birthday.

4. I had a ____________ score on my last test so I had to take it again.

5. Blind _________ could lead you to cutting corners on your way to success.

Match the word with the one that shows its opposite meaning

1. Ambition	**a)** Apathy
2. Initiative	**b)** Indifference
3. Enthusiasm	**c)** Extraneous
4. Exaggerate	**d)** Lethargy
5. Pertinent	**e)** Understate

Unit 05. Resume and Cover Letter

Conversation Questions

1. What experiences do you have on your resume?
2. Because computers check a lot of resumes nowadays,
   how can you optimize your resume for success?
3. Is it okay to exaggerate on your resume?
4. Is there a difference between a lie and a white lie?
5. What kind of resume is more suitable for you, chronological or functional?
6. Would you consider hiring someone to write your resume? Why or why not?
7. Is it okay to ask for a photograph on the resume?
   Why is a photograph needed in Korea?
8. Is it okay to ask for your religion, sexual orientation, or family background
   on the resume?

Assignment

Write a sentence using each of the key vocabulary word and idiom given above.

Vocabulary

1.
2.
3.
4.
5.
6.
7.
8.
9.
10.
11.
12.
13.
14.
15.
16.
17.
18.
19.
20.

21.

22.

23.

24.

Idioms

1.

2.

3.

4.

Project ideas

Draft a cover letter and resume for the company you would like to work with.

Definition of Key Words

- **Killer** n. one that kills; one that has a forceful, violent, or striking impact;
  The chemical is used as a weed killer.

- **Killer** adj. causing death or destruction; very impressive or appealing; very difficult;
  Crossfit is a killer exercise program to help you lose weight.
  Synonyms: fatal, deadly, lethal, terminal, vital
  Origin: first known use in the 15th century

- **Scrutinize** v. to examine something carefully especially in a critical way;
  I closely scrutinized my opponent's every move.
  Synonyms: audit, examine, overlook, oversee, survey
  Origin: first known use in 1671

- **Revise** n. an act of revising; a printing proof that incorporates changes marked in a previous proof;
  That paper needs one more revise.

- **Revise** v. to make changes especially to correct or improve something; to study something again;
  I would like to revise my estimate.
  Synonyms: alter, modify, recast, rework, revamp
  Origin: first known use in 1596

- **Peruse** v. to look at or read something in an informal or relaxed way;
  to examine or read in a very careful way; *He perused the newspaper over breakfast.*
  Synonyms: read, pore over
  Origin: Middle English, from Latin, first known use in 1532

- **Measured** adj. done with thought and care; *This crisis requires a measured response.*
  Synonyms: advised, calculated, considered, knowing, deliberate
  Origin: first known use in the 14th century

- **Pertinent** adj. relating to the thing that is being thought about or discussed;
  He impressed the jury with his concise, pertinent answers to the attorney's questions.
  Synonyms: applicable, germane, material, relative, relevant
  Origin: Middle English, from Anglo-French, first known use in the 14th century

Unit 05. Resume and Cover Letter

- **Hierarchy** n. a group that controls an organization and is divided into different levels;
a system in which people or things are placed in a series of levels with different importance or status; *He was at the bottom of the corporate hierarchy.*
Origin: first known use in the 14th century

- **Exaggerate** v. to think of or describe something as larger or greater than it really is;
to make something larger or greater than normal;
It is impossible to exaggerate the importance of this discovery.
Synonyms: color, elaborate, embellish, magnify, stretch
Origin: first known use in 1613

- **Reference** n. the act of mentioning something in speech or in writing; the act of looking at or in something for information; a person who can be asked for information about another person's character, abilities, etc.

- **Reference** adj. used to find information about something; *He has the list of reference materials.*

- **Reference** v. to supply with references; *The book references many other authors.*
Synonyms: authority, source
Origin: first known use in 1891.

- **Advice** n. an opinion or suggestion about what someone should do; *He needs advice from an expert.*
Synonyms: adjuration, admonition, counsel, guidance, input
Origin: first known use in 14th century

- **Tandem** n. a group of two people or things that work together or are associated with each other;
The team has a tandem of talented guards.

- **Tandem** adv. one after or behind another

- **Tandem** adj. consisting of things or having parts arranged one behind the other
Origin: Latin, first known use in 1785

- **Tailor** n. a person who makes men's clothes that are measured to fit a particular person

- **Tailor** v. to make clothing that is measured to fit a particular person;
  to make or change something so that it meets a special need or purpose;
  I had my suit tailored.
  Synonyms: acclimate, accommodate, adjust, conform, shape
  Origin: first known use in 1719

- **Exemplary** adj. extremely good and deserving to be admired and copied; serving as an example of something;
  Bill Clinton gave exemplary service to the country.
  Synonyms: classic, definitive, imitable, quintessential
  Origin: first known use in 1507

- **Initiative** n. the power or opportunity to do something before others do; the energy and desire that is needed to do something; a plan or program that is intended to solve a problem;
  The governor proposed a new initiative to improve education in urban schools.
  Synonyms: action, ambition, hustle, enterprise
  Origin: first known use in 1793

pp. 56~60 한국어 해설

이력서와 자기소개서

주요단어 및 구절

1. 죽이는 / 죽여주는
2. 세심히 살피다 / 보다
3. 실망한
4. 보통 이하의
5. 수정하다 / 검토하다
6. 정독하다
7. 측정된 / 측정한
8. 경험이 있는 / 노련한
9. 순서대로
10. 기능적인
11. 적절한 / 관련된
12. 우선순위 / 계급
13. 수량화할 수 있는
14. 과장하다
15. 추천인
16. 충고
17. 2인용 자전거 / 앞뒤 한 줄로 / 나란한 (in tandem ~와 동시에)
18. 교정하다
19. 모범적인
20. 열정
21. 결단력
22. 포부
23. 거짓말하는 것은 도덕상 옳지 않는
24. 주변 사람들과 관련이 있다 / 주변 사람들에게 영향을 미치다

숙어 및 표현

1. 단도직입적인
2. 모로 가도 서울만 가면 된다
3. 사실을 날조하다
4. 매우 흔한 / 매우 싼

빈칸 채우기

1. Killer
2. Quantifiable
3. Disappointed
4. Sub-par
5. Ambition

반대의 의미 단어 찾기

1. d
2. b
3. a
4. e
5. c

대화 질문

1. 어떤 경험들을 이력서에 적었는가?
2. 요즘에는 컴퓨터가 많은 이력서들을 확인하고 있기 때문에, 당신은 성공하기 위하여 어떻게 이력서를 최적화 할 수 있는가?
3. 이력을 과장해도 괜찮은가?
4. 거짓말과 선의의 거짓말은 서로 다른가?
5. 연대순 배열 이력서와 기능 중심적 이력서 중에 어떤 것이 당신에게 잘 맞는가?
6. 당신의 이력서를 쓰게 하기 위해 누군가를 고용할 것인가? 그렇다면(왜?) 그렇지 않다면(왜?)
7. 이력서에 증명사진을 요구하는게 괜찮은가? 왜 한국에서는 이력서에 증명사진이 필요한가?
8. 이력서에 종교, 성적 기호 혹은 가정환경을 요구하는 것이 괜찮은가?

과제

위에 주어진 단어와 숙어를 가지고 문장을 만드시오.

프로젝트 아이디어

당신이 일하고 싶은 회사에 낼 이력서와 자기소개서를 작성해 보아라.

Unit 06

The Job Interview

Your resume and cover letter are good. You feel like everything is in the bag. Then your dream employer calls you for the interview, and now you find yourself in the hot seat. You have butterflies in your stomach, your palms are sweaty, and your voice is weak. However, there is no need to fret if you have practiced and prepared. Here are some tips to make your interview a piece of cake.

Body Language: Be aware of your posture. If you slouch, you look lazy. If you sit tall with your chest protruding, you will not only look more confident but also feel it as your brain releases endorphins to follow your body's actions. Do not offer your hand first for a handshake. Let the interviewer extend his/her hand, smile and then shake the hand. During the interview, maintain eye contact because if you turn your eyes away, it will appear as though you are hiding something. Finally, do not cross your legs and nod along in agreement so that you do not appear to be distracted or uninterested.

Anticipation: In all likelihood, the employer probably only cares about your health, intelligence, aptitude, and circumstances. The employer just wants to make sure you are physically and mentally capable of working, and have the right skill-sets for the job. In addition, the employer wants to know when you can begin work and whether you can stick around. But to see if you are really sharp as a tack, he/she may even ask some questions to test your resolve.

No matter how wacky the questions are, be in your own element. To do that, make a list of five achievements, five skill-sets you possess, five things you are good at, or five things that you are proud of having achieved at school or at work. If you do this, you will not have cold feet when you are bombarded with all sorts of questions. Just bring the question to one of your strengths. Even then, the interview can be challenging because of oddball questions that force candidates to think on their feet. Try to practice questions from out of left field to be ready for any circumstance.

- Key Vocabulary
- Idioms and Expressions

해석

취업 면접

당신의 이력서와 자기소개서가 좋다. 당신은 모든 것이 확실하다고 느낀다. 그리고는 당신의 이상적인 고용인은 전화해서 인터뷰를 보러 오라고 한다. 이제 당신은 곤란한 입장에 처한 자신을 발견한다. 당신은 긴장돼서 속이 울렁거리고 손바닥에 땀이 나고 당신의 목소리는 약하다. 그러나 충분히 연습하고 준비했다면 조마조마할 필요가 없다. 여기 면접을 쉽게 볼 수 있는 몇 가지 팁들을 알려주겠다.

보디랭귀지 (몸짓언어) : 자세를 의식해라. 구부정하면 게을러 보인다. 만약 허리를 펴고 가슴을 내밀고 앉으면 자신만만해 보일 뿐만 아니라 너의 몸동작을 따르려고 뇌가 엔도르핀을 분비함에 따라 자신감이 생기는 것 또한 느낄 수 있을 것이다. 그리고 악수하려 먼저 손을 뻗지 마라. 면접관이 먼저 손을 뻗으면 그때 웃으면서 악수해라. 인터뷰가 진행되는 동안 면접관과 계속 시선을 마주쳐라. 만약 시선을 돌리면 당신이 무언가 숨기는게 있다고 보여질 수 있다. 마지막으로 동의할 때 다리를 꼰 채로 고개를 끄덕거리지마라. 당신이 산만하거나 무관심해 보이지 않게 하기 위해서이다.

기대 : 십중팔구 고용자들은 당신의 건강, 지능, 소질 그리고 환경에만 신경을 쓸 것이다. 고용자들은 당신이 신체적, 정신적으로 일을 감당해 낼 수 있으며 일에 알맞은 기술이 있는지 확인하고 싶어 한다. 게다가 고용자들은 당신이 일을 시작하고 오래 머물 수 있는지를 알고 싶어 한다. 그러나 당신이 정말 똑똑한지 아닌지 알기 위해 그들은 너의 결의를 보려고 질문을 할 수 있다.

질문이 아무리 터무니없어도 당신 자신을 유지해라. 그러기 위해 당신의 다섯 가지의 업적, 다섯 가지의 기술, 당신이 잘하는 다섯 가지, 혹은 학교나 직장에서 당신이 성취했기에 자랑스러운 다섯 가지의 목록을 만들어라. 이것을 한다면, 당신은 어떤 질문 폭격을 받아도 무섭지 않을 것이다. 질문을 너의 장점들 중 하나로 이끌어 답하여라. 그렇다 하더라도, 면접은 임기응변을 강요하는 괴짜 질문들 때문에 매우 힘들 수 있다. 어떠한 경우라도 준비되어 있기 위해 예상치 못한 질문들을 연습해라.

Unit 06. The Job Interview

Key Vocabulary and Phrases

1. Fret
2. Posture
3. Slouch
4. Lazy
5. Protruding
6. Distracted
7. Aptitude
8. Circumstances
9. Wacky
10. Bombarded
11. In all likelihood
12. Stick around
13. Hot seat
14. Resolve
15. Oddball
16. Endorphin

Idioms and Expressions

1. Everything is in the bag
2. Butterflies in your stomach
3. Piece of cake
4. Sharp as a tack
5. Cold feet
6. In your own element
7. Out of left field

Unit 06. The Job Interview

Fill in the blanks with the appropriate word

1. Everyone has tough ______________; what is important is how you overcome them.

2. If you are __________, you probably will not ever become rich.

3. The famous athlete was ____________ with questions after he was found guilty of using steroids.

4. He wants to become an engineer since he has a high ____________ in math.

5. If you __________ on your office desk, you may develop shoulder problems.

Match the word with the one that shows its opposite meaning

1. Distract	**a)** Delay
2. Wacky	**b)** Sane
3. Resolve	**c)** Compress
4. Protrude	**d)** Compose
5. Lazy	**e)** Industrious

Wacky Job Interview Questions

1. How honest are you?
2. What is your least favorite thing about humanity?
3. Why is a tennis ball fuzzy?
4. If you were 80 years old, what would you tell your children?
5. What is the color of money?
6. Describe to me the process and benefits of wearing a seatbelt.
7. If you were a box of cereal, what would you be and why?
8. If you were on an island and could only bring three things, what would you bring?
9. Do you believe in aliens?
10. Are you more of a hunter or a gatherer?

Assignment

Write a sentence using each of the key vocabulary word and idiom given above.

Vocabulary

1. ______________________________
2. ______________________________
3. ______________________________
4. ______________________________
5. ______________________________

6.

7.

8.

9.

10.

11.

12.

13.

14.

15.

16.

Idioms

1.

2.

3.

4.

5.

6.

7.

Class Idea

Form different teams with one interviewer and three candidates. Move around to different groups and conduct a mock job interview.

Explore Further

On YouTube listen to the TED talk by Anna Post

Put Those Smartphones Away: Great Tips for Making Your Job Interview Count

Definition of Key Words

- **Fret** v. to eat or gnaw into; to become vexed or worried; to become agitated;
  Do not fret about the economy; *We are just going through another business cycle.*
  Origin: Middle English, from Old English, first known use in the 12th century

- **Posture** n. The way in which your body is positioned when you are sitting or standing;
  the attitude a person or group has toward a subject; *Humans have an upright posture.*
  Synonyms: attitude, poise, stance, station

- **Slouch** n. a way of walking, sitting, or standing with the head and shoulders bent forward;
  a lazy or worthless person; *She's no slouch at yoga.*
  Synonyms: couch potato, deadbeat, loafer, slug, sluggard
  Origin: first known use in 1515

- **Protrude** v. to stick out; *His lower jaw protrudes slightly.*
  Synonyms: bag, balloon, bulge, stand out, swell
  Origin: first known use in 1620

Unit 06. The Job Interview

- **Distract** v. — to cause someone to stop thinking about or paying attention to someone or something and to think about or pay attention to someone or something else instead;
  to take attention away from someone or something; *He was distracted from his studies.*
  Synonyms: abstract, call off, detract, divert, throw off
  Origin: Middle English, from Latin, first known use in the 14th century

- **Aptitude** n. — a natural ability to do something or to learn something;
  The new test is supposed to measure the aptitude of the students.
  Synonyms: affection, affinity, inclination, penchant, predilection, propensity
  Origin: Middle English, from Medieval Latin, first known use in the 15th century

- **Circumstances** n. — a condition or fact that affects a situation; the way something happens;
  the specific details of an event; *He was a victim of circumstances.*
  Synonyms: fate, destiny, doom, fortune, portion
  Origin: first known use in the 13th century

- **Wacky** adj. — amusing and very strange; *My wacky aunt owns thirty cats.*
  Synonyms: bizarre, cranky, eccentric, erratic, far-out
  Origin: first known use in 1935

- **Resolve** v. — to find an answer or solution to something;
  to make a definite and serious decision to do something;
  to make a formal decision about something usually by a vote;
  The brothers finally resolved their conflict.
  Synonyms: choose, conclude, determine, figure, settle

- **Resolve** n. — a strong determination to do something; *He was unwavering in his resolve to become rich.*
  Origin: first known use in 1591

- **Endorphin** n. — peptides found especially in the brain that bind chiefly to opiate receptors and produce some pharmacological effects like pain relief;
  Running releases the endorphins responsible for the creation of happiness.
  Origin: first known use in 1976

pp. 67~69 한국어 해설

면접

주요단어 및 구절

1. 조마조마하다
2. 자세
3. 구부정한
4. 게으른
5. 튀어나오다
6. 산만한
7. 소질
8. 환경
9. 괴짜의 / 터무니없는
10. 공세를 받는, 퍼부어지는
11. 십중팔구
12. 머무르다
13. 어려운 상황에 처한
14. 결의 / 해결하다
15. 괴짜
16. 엔도르핀

숙어와 표현

1. 틀림없다 / 확실하다
2. 몹시 긴장하다
   (긴장해서 속이 울렁거린다, 긴장해서 가슴이 두근거린다)
3. 몹시 쉬운(누워서 떡 먹기)
4. 예리한, 머리회전이 빠른
5. 겁 / 긴장
6. 자신을 유지하는
7. 뜻밖에

빈칸 채우기

1. Circumstances
2. Lazy
3. Bombarded
4. Aptitude
5. Slouch

반대의 의미 단어 찾기

1. d
2. b
3. a
4. c
5. e

괴짜 면접질문

1. 당신은 얼마나 정직한가?
2. 당신이 가장 싫어하는 인간성은 무엇인가?
3. 테니스 볼은 왜 솜털이 보송보송한가?
4. 당신이 만약 80세가 되었을 때, 너의 자식들에게 뭐라고 말하겠는가?
5. 돈은 무슨 색깔인가?
6. 안전벨트를 차는 과정과 이익을 설명하라.
7. 당신이 만약 시리얼 상자라면, 무엇이 되고 싶은가? 왜?
8. 만약 세 가지만을 무인도에 가져갈 수 있다면, 무엇을 가져가겠는가?
9. 외계인을 믿는가?
10. 당신은 수렵 꾼 혹은 채집꾼 중 무엇에 더 가깝나?

과제

위의 주어진 단어와 숙어를 가지고 문장을 만드시오.

수업 아이디어

1명의 면접관과 3명의 후보자들이 다른 팀에 들어가 서로 돌아가며 모의면접을 진행하시오.

Module 02.

Doing well at work 직장에서 일 잘하기

Unit 07

Business Etiquette

Having etiquette is an essential skill for today's job market. It is not rocket science, but many people are unskilled at it. The devil is in the details. Think about it. If you are a CEO, would you hire someone who dresses however he/she wants or chews food with his/her mouth open? Probably not because the employee is a representative of the firm. So you better believe that having good etiquette is critical to your success. Although not exhaustive, here are a few other tips to bear in mind.

Appearance: Body odor and bad breath are no-brainers. It is also important not to twitch your foot during meetings or to have a sloppy posture. Ensure that your dress and style are as professional as your communication. You do not want to screw up and have people say behind your back, "I can't believe he just did that."

Greeting: In many Western countries, maintaining direct eye contact and greeting with a firm handshake are typically seen as good manners. In contrast, in some Asian countries, it is considered rude to look someone directly in the eye or shake the hand in a rough manner. Here you will have to strike a balance depending on whom you meet and where you are. Either way, having a good smile is one of the hallmarks of a good greeting.

Business Cards: Business cards are a statement of who you are and who you want to be. Some make their cards memorable by using both sides or having a good design. Nowadays, firms such as Evernote even allow you to take photos of business cards, which automatically link with your LinkedIn account, a famous American networking website. While in Korea, there are some particular rules to follow: (1) stand up when you exchange cards, (2) receive cards with both hands, and (3) make sure not to tuck cards into your wallet right away but rather keep them in front of you on the table for the duration of the meeting.

Dining: Dress nicely if you are at an expensive restaurant. Do not put your cell phone or keys on the table or take pictures of the food, unless you are just following the clients to make them feel comfortable. Moreover, do not discuss business until at least the conclusion of the main course. Remember that Koreans like to drink. If you are with Korean hosts, it is considered rude to refuse a drink or to pour your own. If someone's cup is empty, you can pour him/her a drink but ensure that you use both the hands. The importance of drinking in Korea cannot be understated; it is a way for everyone to bond together and form a relationship. If you are drinking out, certainly have fun but do not be a loose cannon because that can be considered uncouth behavior.

- Key Vocabulary
- Idioms and Expressions

해석

비즈니스 에티켓

예의를 갖춘다는 것은 오늘날 취업시장에서 필수 기술이다. 어려운 기술은 아니지만 많은 사람들이 능숙하지 않다. 악마는 사소한 곳에 있는 법이다. 생각해봐라. 당신이 CEO라면 자기 마음대로 옷을 입는 사람 그리고 입을 벌리며 음식을 씹는 사람을 고용하겠는가? 직원은 회사를 대표하기 때문에 아마 고용하지 않을 것이다. 그러므로 당신의 성공을 위하여 바른 예의를 갖는 것이 매우 중요하다는 틀림없다. 총망라한 것은 아니지만 여기 당신이 명심해야 할 몇 개 팁들이 있다.

외모 : 체취나 입 냄새는 쉬운 문제이다. 그러나 회의 때 다리를 떨지 않는 것, 단정히 앉은 자세는 중요하다. 그리고 너의 옷차림과 스타일이 말만큼 전문적이도록 확실히 하라. 당신은 일을 망치고 사람들이 당신 뒤에서 "그런 일을 했다는 것을 믿을 수 없어"라고 수군대는 것을 원하지 않을 것이다.

인사 : 눈을 맞춘 상태를 지속하는 것과 상대의 손을 꽉 쥐는 악수로 인사를 하는 것은 서양의 많은 나라들에서 좋은 매너로 생각한다. 반대로 몇몇 아시아 나라들에서는 다른 사람의 눈을 똑바로 보는 것이나 거친 악수는 무례하다고 생각한다. 당신이 누구를 만나는지 어디에 있는지에 따라 균형을 잘 맞춰야 한다. 어느 쪽이든 좋은 미소를 짓는 것은 좋은 인사의 특징이다.

명함 : 명함은 당신이 누구인지 그리고 누가 되고 싶은지에 대한 진술이다. 어떤 사람들은 양면을 사용하거나 좋은 디자인을 통해 기억할 만한 명함을 만든다. 요즘, Evernote와 같은 회사는 심지어 명함을 찍어서 자동으로 미국의 유명한 네트워크 인맥 사이트인 링크드인 계정에 연결해주기도 한다. 반면에 한국은 따라야 할 특별한 규칙들이 있다. (1) 명함을 교환할 때는 서서 한다. (2) 두 손으로 명함을 받는다. 그리고 (3) 명함을 받은 후 바로 지갑에 집어넣지 말고 회의가 진행되는 동안 자기 앞의 책상 위에 올려놓는다.

식사 : 당신이 만약 비싼 식당에 간다면 옷을 잘 입어야 한다. 고객의 행동을 따라 하여 고객을 편안하게 만들려는 게 아니라면 핸드폰이나 열쇠를 테이블 위에 놓지 말고 음식 사진을 찍지 말아라. 더 나아가 최소한 주메뉴 요리가 끝날 때까지는 사업에 대하여 논의하지 마라. 한국인들은 술을 좋아하는 것을 기억해라. 만약 한국인 주최자와 함께 있다면 술을 거절하거나 스스로 따라 마시는 것은 무례하다고 여겨진다. 만약 다른 사람의 잔이 비었다면 술을 따라줄 수 있지만 두 손을 사용해 따라줘야 한다. 한국에서 술의 중요성은 과소평가될 수 없다; 이것은 모두 결합하고 인맥을 맺는 수단이다. 만약 당신이 밖에서 술을 마신다면 최대한 즐기되 보기 흉한 행동으로 생각될 수 있는 돌발행동을 하는 사람은 되지 마라.

Unit 07. Business Etiquette

Key Vocabulary and Phrases

1. Etiquette
2. Essential
3. Exhaustive
4. Professional
5. Rough
6. Hallmark
7. Particular
8. Tuck
9. Understated
10. Bond
11. Critical
12. Sloppy
13. You better believe ...
14. No-brainer
15. Uncouth

Idioms and Expressions

1. It is not rocket science
2. The devil is in the details
3. Screw up
4. Loose cannon

Fill in the blanks with the appropriate word

1. He has __________ tastes when it comes to selecting wine.
2. The __________ between a parent and a child lasts forever.
3. She got an F on her homework because no one could understand her __________ handwriting.
4. It is __________ to attend Harvard if you got accepted.
5. My mom used to always tell me to __________ my shirt in before going to church.

Unit 07. Business Etiquette

Match the word with the one that shows its opposite meaning

1. Critical	**a)** Needless
2. Sloppy	**b)** Amateur
3. Essential	**c)** Undemanding
4. Professional	**d)** Flamboyant
5. Understated	**e)** Dashing

Conversation Questions

1. What clothes are suitable for the office? Should you overdress or underdress?

2. How do many Asians wear suits in the summer without sweating?

3. Explain the differences in body language between foreigners and Koreans when they greet.

4. Describe someone you know who has impeccable manners and etiquette.
How does he/she behave?

5. Do foreigners and Koreans treat business cards differently?

6. Can you explain the Korean drinking culture and all of its rules?

7. What are some good excuses to refuse a drink with Koreans at a business meeting?

8. In Korea, what behaviors of the foreigners is considered rude by the locals?

9. What customs or practices are found only in Korea? Or only in the U.S.?

10. Which country has the most polite culture?

Assignment

Write a sentence using each of the key vocabulary word and idiom given above.

Vocabulary

1.

2.

3.

4.

5.

6.

7.

8.

9.

10.

11.

12.

13.

14.

15.

Unit 07. Business Etiquette

Idioms

1.

2.

3.

4.

Presentation Idea

Give a group presentation on the etiquette foreigners need to know before doing business in Korea.

Explore Further

On YouTube listen to the TED talk by Evan Selinger

Digital Age Etiquette

Presentation Idea

Give a group presentation on the etiquette foreigners need to know before doing business in Korea.

Definition of Key Words

- **Etiquette** n. rules indicating the proper and polite way to behave; *The couple exhibited poor etiquette when they left the party without saying good-bye to the host and hostess.*
  Synonyms: manner, form, mores, proprieties
  Origin: French, first known use in 1750

- **Essential** adj. extremely important and necessary; very basic; *Free speech is essential to democracy.*

- **Essential** n. something that is basic or necessary; something essential;
  The essentials for success include having the right attitude.
  Synonyms: condition, demand, necessary, necessity, requisite
  Origin: first known use in the 15th century

- **Exhaustive** adj. including all possibilities; very thorough; *The list was long but not exhaustive.*
  Synonyms: all-out, comprehensive, full-scale, total
  Origin: first known use in 1789

- **Professional** adj. relating to a job that requires special education, training, or skill; done or given by a person who works in a particular profession; paid to participate in a sport or activity;
  Do you have any professional experience?

- **Professional** n. someone who does a job that requires special training, education, or skill; someone who is a member of a profession; *She handled the situation like a professional.*
  Synonyms: pro, veteran, experienced person
  Origin: first known use in 1811

- **Rough** adj. having a surface that is not even; having or causing sudden, violent movements; difficult or unpleasant to deal with; *They hiked through rough terrain.*
  Synonyms: brushy, hairy, shaggy, bristly
  Origin: Middle English, from Old English, first known use in the 12th century

Unit 07. Business Etiquette

- **Hallmark** n.
  a quality, ability, etc. that is typical of a particular person or thing;
  an official mark that is put on gold and silver objects in Britain to indicate their purity;
  He had all the hallmarks of a great basketball player.
  Synonyms: emblem, logo, symbol, trademark
  Origin: first known use in 1721

- **Particular** adj.
  used to indicate that one specific person or thing is being referred to;
  special or more than usual; having very definite options about what is good or acceptable;
  Pay particular attention to the poet's choice of words.

- **Particular** n.
  a specific detail or piece of information
  Synonyms: detail, item, point
  Origin: first known use in the 15th century

- **Tuck** v.
  to push the end of something into or being something in order to hold it in place, make it look neat, etc.; to put something in a particular place usually to hide it, hold it, or make it safe;
  A bag was tucked under her arm.
  Origin: Middle English, first known use in the 14th century

- **Understated** adj.
  expressed or done in quiet or simple way;
  His understated sense of style is surprisingly fashionable.
  Synonyms: conservative, low-key, subdued, toned-down, unpretentious
  Origin: first known use in 1909

- **Bond** n.
  something such as an idea or interest or experience that is shared between people;
  a chain or rope that is used to prevent someone from moving or acting freely;
  Daughters have a special bond with their mothers.

- **Bond** v.
  to join things together; to form a close relationship with someone;
  Heat was used to bond the sheets of plastic together.
  Synonyms: commune, click, relate
  Origin: first known use in 1677

- **Critical** adj. expressing criticism or disapproval;
  of or relating to the judgments of critics about books, movies, art, etc.;
  careful judgment about the good and bad parts of something;
  She has a talent for critical thinking.
  Synonyms: judgmental, overcritical, faultfinding
  Origin: first known use in 1547

- **Sloppy** adj. not careful or neat; romantic in a foolish or exaggerated way;
  containing or involving a lot of liquid or too much liquid;
  Your work has been very sloppy lately.
  Synonyms: unkempt, untidy, blowsy
  Origin: first known use in 1672

- **Uncouth** adj. behaving in a rude way; not polite or socially acceptable;
  People thought he was uncouth and uncivilized.
  Synonyms: boorish, clownish, classless
  Origin: first known use before the 12th century.

pp. 79~82 한국어 해설

비즈니스 에티켓

주요단어 및 구절

1. 예의, 예절
2. 필수적인
3. 총망라한 / (빠뜨리는 것 없이) 철저한
4. 전문적인
5. 거친
6. 특징
7. 특별한
8. 집어넣다
9. 과소평가된, 무시된
10. 맺다
11. 중요한
12. 엉성한
13. …이 틀림없다
14. 쉬운 문제
15. 보기 흉한

숙어 및 표현

1. 고도의 지능이 요구되는 일은 아니다.
2. 악마는 사소한 것 속에 있다.
3. 망치다
4. 예측불허의 사람, 돌출행동을 하는 사람

빈칸 채우기

1. Particular
2. Bond
3. Sloppy
4. Critical
5. Tuck

반대의 의미 단어 찾기

1. c
2. e
3. a
4. b
5. d

대화 질문

1. 어떤 옷이 사무실에 어울리는가? 차려 입어야 하는가? 간소하게 입어야 하는가?
2. 어떻게 많은 아시안들은 땀 흘리지 않고 여름에 정장을 입는가?
3. 외국인과 한국인이 인사할 때 몸짓언어의 차이점들을 설명하라.
4. 당신이 아는 흠잡을 데 없는 매너와 예절을 가진 사람을 묘사해라. 그들이 어떻게 행동하는가?
5. 외국인들과 한국인들이 명함을 다르게 대하는가?
6. 한국의 음주 문화와 그의 모든 규칙을 설명할 수 있는가?
7. 사업적인 만남에서 한국인들과의 술자리를 거절하기 위한 좋은 변명은 무엇이 있는가?
8. 한국 현지인들에게 무례하다고 생각되는 외국인들의 행동은 무엇이 있는가?
9. 한국에서만 볼 수 있는 관습이나 관례는 무엇인가? 미국에서만 볼 수 있는 예절은?
10. 어느 나라 문화가 가장 예의바른가?

과제

위에 주어진 단어와 숙어를 가지고 문장을 만드시오.

발표아이디어

한국에서 사업하기 전에 외국인이 알아야 할 예절에 대해 조별 발표를 하여라.

Unit 08

Negotiating Effectively

Negotiation is a dialogue between two or more people to resolve differences, reach understanding, or gain some sort of advantage. Negotiation happens because of conflicts. Conflict comes from some sort of interdependency among people, where one person's decisions may affect another. As poet John Donne wrote, "No man is an island." The best scenario for all involved is a win–win situation, but it is not always possible. At work, at home, and with our friends and family, having negotiation skills can help us navigate our way toward success.

The ability to influence others or win them over is often very helpful in negotiating. Dale Carnegie in his book "How to Win Friends and Influence People" gives some interesting advice. He says the first thing is to listen carefully. It is true; even if you have got the gift of gab, scientists have found that listeners are more influential than talkers. In addition, make sure to smile genuinely and make eye contact but not for too long. Staring into someone's eyes can suggest that you are trying to stare them down or exert dominance, which is a clear no–no if you are looking to influence. Morever, it gets on everyone's nerves when someone is wrong but does not apologize. Apologize sparingly, but if you are wrong, make sure you admit it.

Another bit of advice is for a common negotiation situation. Who should make the first offer? One psychological theory called the anchoring principle says that if you want the upper hand, you should be the first to make the offer. Take a salary negotiation: whoever makes the first offer has the chance to establish the range of possible salaries as determined by the initial or anchoring offer. If you start high, the hiring manager may ask you to accept something slightly lower. However if the manager makes the initial low-ball offer, you might be inclined to accept something just a little bit higher. Therefore the next time you negotiate, be the first to drop the anchor down on the table.

Lastly, understand that negotiation styles vary around the globe. This information is a bit stereotypical, but it is meant to shed light on how cultures affect negotiation style. For instance, the Swiss tend to be straightforward and logical while the Japanese may be more indirect about what is acceptable or not. Somewhat similarly, Koreans may be indirect but are ardent conversationalists who may insist on building some goodwill before any deal goes down.

- Key Vocabulary
- Idioms and Expressions

해석

효율적으로 협상하기

협상은 차이를 해결하기 위하여, 이해를 하기 위하여 혹은, 어떤 이익을 얻기 위하여 둘 또는 그 이상의 사람들 사이에서 하는 대화이다. 협상은 갈등 때문에 생긴다. 갈등은 한 사람의 결정이 다른 사람들에게 영향을 끼칠 수 있는 사람들 사이의 상호의존성에서 생긴다. 시인 John Donne에 따르면 "아무도 혼자인 사람은 없다." 연관된 모두에게 가장 좋은 시나리오는 win-win하는 것이다. 그러나 항상 가능하진 않다. 직장에서, 집에서, 친구들 그리고 가족과 하는 협상 기술은 우리에게 성공으로 향하는 길 찾기를 도와준다.

다른 사람에게 영향을 미치거나 설득하는 능력은 협상에 몹시 도움이 된다. 데일 카네기는 그의 저서 〈친구를 얻고 사람들에게 영향력을 행사하는 방법〉에서 흥미로운 충고를 해준다. 첫 번째는 주의 깊게 듣는 것이라고 그는 말한다. 그것은 맞다. 당신이 말재주가 많다고 하더라도, 과학자들은 청자(듣는 사람)들이 화자(말하는 사람)들보다 더 많은 영향력을 끼친다는 것을 발견했다. 추가적으로, 당신이 진실된 미소를 짓고 눈 맞춤을 하되 너무 오래 하지 않는 것을 명심해라. 누군가의 눈을 응시하는 것은 당신이 그들을 노려보아 눈길을 피하게 만드는 것이거나 권력을 행사하는 것임을 암시할 수 있다. 당신이 영향을 끼치려 한다면 정말 안 되는 행동이다. (당신이 영향을 주려 한다고 하면 정말 안 되는 행동인 누군가의 눈을 응시하는 것은 그들을 노려보아 눈길을 피하게 만드는 것이거나 권력을 행사하는 것이다.) 그리고 잘못하고 사과를 안 하는 것은 모든 이의 신경을 거슬리게 한다. 사과를 삼가되, 잘못을 했다면 꼭 인정해야 한다.

다른 약간의 충고는 일반적인 협상 상황을 위한 것이다. 누가 먼저 제안을 해야 하는가? 정착 원칙이라고 하는 심리학 이론은 당신이 우위를 점하고 싶으면, 당신이 먼저 제안을 해야 한다고 한다. 급여 협상을 예로 들면: 누구든지 먼저 제시하는 사람이 최초나 마무리 제안으로 결정되는 급여 가능 범위를 정할 기회가 있다. 만약 당신이 높은 액수로 시작하면, 고용 매니저는 너에게 약간 낮은 액수로 받아들이길 청할 것이다. 그러나 만약 고용 매니저가 처음 낮은 임금을 제시한다면 너는 단지 조금 더 높은 액수를 받아들여야 할 것이다. 그러니 다음에 당신이 협상할 때에는, 처음으로 닻을 테이블 위에 내리는 사람이 되어라.

마지막으로, 협상 방식은 전 세계적으로 다르다는 것을 이해하라. 이 정보는 약간 틀에 박힌 것 일수도 있지만 협상 방식에 문화가 얼마나 많은 영향을 미치는지 알려주고자 하는 것이다. 예를 들어 일본인들은 무엇이 수용 가능한지 아닌지에 대하여 간접적인 반면, 스위스 사람들은 논리적이고 솔직한 경향이 있다. 어느 정도 비슷하게, 한국인들은 간접적일 수도 있지만 거래가 성립되기 전에 호의를 쌓는 것을 주장하는 열렬한 대화자들이다.

Unit 08. Negotiating Effectively

Key Vocabulary and Phrases

1. Conflict
2. Interdependency
3. Scenario
4. Negotiation
5. Navigate
6. Influence
7. Genuinely
8. Staring
9. Exert
10. Dominance
11. Inclined
12. Stereotype
13. Goodwill
14. Conversationalist
15. Win-win situation
16. Gift of gab
17. Clear no–no
18. Anchoring principle

Idioms and Expressions

1. No man is an island
2. Low-ball offer
3. Having the upper hand
4. Getting on someone's nerves
5. Shedding light on something

Fill in the blanks with the appropriate word

1. Conflicts usually happen because there is some ______________.

2. In a war ___________ on the Korean peninsula, millions of people can lose their lives.

3. My father has great ___________ on my choice of career.

4. The racist man believed in all the negative _____________.

5. Some people ______________ care for others and want to help others out.

Match the word with the one that shows its opposite meaning

1. Stare	**a)** Venom
2. Influence	**b)** Idle
3. Navigate	**c)** Get
4. Goodwill	**d)** Impotence
5. Exert	**e)** Glimpse

Unit 08. Negotiating Effectively

Conversation Questions

1. What negotiations do you have with your parents?
2. What negotiations do you have at work?
3. What are some key tips on being a good negotiator?
4. Have you ever resolved some conflict between two people? How did it go?
5. Describe a win-win situation that you have been in.
6. Who is the most persuasive among your friends? Describe his/her personality.
7. Is the anchoring principle a reliable scientific fact?
8. Describe how different cultures negotiate differently.
9. Can violent conflicts be solved with violence?
10. When is war justified?

Assignment

Write a sentence using each of the key vocabulary word and idiom given above.

Vocabulary

1. ______________________________

2. ______________________________

3. ______________________________

4.

5.

6.

7.

8.

9.

10.

11.

12.

13.

14.

15.

16.

17.

18.

Idioms

1.

2.

3.

4.

5.

Unit 08. Negotiating Effectively

Class Idea

Divide into groups representing different countries. Then negotiate some global conflict such as the peaceful reunification on the Korean peninsula. Negotiate a win-win for all sides.

Explore Further

On YouTube listen to the TED talk by William Ury

The Walk from "No" to "Yes"

Definition of Key Words

- **Conflict** n. — a struggle for power; strong disagreement between people;
  I don't have any conflicts between the theories.

- **Conflict** v. — to be different in a way that prevents agreement;
  to say or express opposite things; to happen at the same time as something else;
  Reports conflicted on how many people were involved.
  Synonyms: collide, clash, disaccord, discord, jar
  Origin: first known use in the 15th century

- **Scenario** n. — a description of what could possibly happen; a written description of a plan, movie, opera, etc.;
  A possible scenario would be that we move to the city.
  Synonyms: screenplay, script
  Origin: first known use in 1875

- **Negotiation** n. — a formal discussion between people who are trying to reach an agreement;
  an act of negotiating; *She is skilled at negotiation.*
  Synonyms: accommodation, compromise, give-and-take; concession
  Origin: first known use in the 15th century

- **Navigate** v. — to find the way to get to a place when you are traveling in a ship, airplane, car, etc.;
  to sail on, over, or through an area of water; *I'd need a map to navigate the city.*
  Synonyms: helm, pilot, steer
  Origin: first known use in 1588

- **Influence** n. the power to change or affect someone or something;
a person or thing that affects someone or something in an important way;
Her parents still have a great deal of influence over her.
Synonyms: authority, clout, credit, juice, sway
Origin: Middle English, from Old French, first known use in the 14th century

- **Genuine** adj. actual, real or true; sincere and honest;
He has a genuine desire to help others.
Synonyms: bona fide, certified, authentic, right
Origin: Latin, first known use in 1639

- **Exert** v. to use strength, ability, etc.; to cause to have an effect or to be felt;
The machine exerted great force.
Synonyms: apply, exercise, ply, wield
Origin: Latin, first known use in 1630

- **Dominant** adj. more important, powerful, or successful than most or all others;
The company is now dominant in its market.
Synonyms: foremost, grand, greatest, highest, number one
Origin: Middle French or Latin, first known use in 1532

- **Inclined** adj. wanting to do something or likely to do something;
having an interest in or a talent for something; *Some people are inclined toward volunteering.*
Synonyms: amenable, disposed, willing, ready
Origin: first known use in the 14th century

- **Stereotype** n. an often unfair and untrue belief that many people have about all people or things
with a particular characteristic; *He is like the stereotype of an absentminded professor.*
Synonyms: conception, generality, notion, generalization
Origin: French, first known use in 1817

- **Goodwill** n. a kind, helpful, or friendly feeling or attitude; business: the amount of value
that a company's good reputation adds to its overall value;
She has goodwill toward all her coworkers.
Synonyms: benevolence, brotherhood, charity, fellowship, kindliness
Origin: before the 12th century

pp. 90~94 한국어 해설

효율적으로 협상하기

주요단어 및 구절

1. 갈등
2. 상호의존
3. 시나리오
4. 협상
5. 길을 찾다
6. 영향
7. 진정으로
8. 응시하는
9. 행사하다, 가하다
10. 권력
11. 하고 싶은, 마음이 기울다
12. 선입견, 고정관념, 편견
13. 호의
14. 대화에 능한 사람
15. 윈윈 상황
16. 말솜씨
17. 하면 정말 안 되는 행동
18. 정착이론

숙어 및 표현

1. 아무도 혼자인 사람은 없다
2. 낮은 견적 제시
3. 이기다, 우세하다
4. ~의 신경을 건드리는[기]
5. ~을 밝히는[기], 알려주는[기]

빈칸 채우기

1. Interdependency
2. Scenario
3. Influence
4. Stereotypes
5. Genuinely

반대의 의미 단어 찾기

1. e
2. d
3. c
4. a
5. b

대화 질문들

1. 당신의 부모님과는 어떤 협상을 하는가?
2. 당신의 직장에서는 어떤 협상을 하는가?
3. 좋은 협상가가 되기 위해서 좋은 팁은 무엇인가?
4. 다른 두 명 사이의 갈등을 해결해 본 적이 있는가? 어땠는가?
5. 당신이 경험한 윈윈 상황을 설명해보라.
6. 당신의 친구들 중 누가 가장 설득력이 있는가? 그들의 성격을 설명해보라.
7. 정착원칙이 믿을만한 과학적 사실인가?
8. 다른 문화들은 어떻게 다르게 협상하는지 설명해보라.
9. 폭력적 갈등이 폭력으로 해결될 수 있는가?
10. 전쟁은 언제 정당화될까?

과제

위에 주어진 단어와 숙어를 가지고 문장을 만드시오.

수업 아이디어

다양한 나라별 그룹을 만들어라. 그리고 한반도의 평화적 통일과 같은 국제적 갈등을 두고 협상하라. 윈윈이 되도록 협상하라.

Unit 09

Presenting Well

You have the greatest idea in the world. However if you cannot explain and persuade others, it might not even matter. In the book "The Presentation Secrets of Steve Jobs," some advice is given on how to present like Steve Jobs. During his tenure at Apple, Jobs introduced the iPhone, iPod, and iPad. These products started whole new product categories with competitors scrambling in to get in on the action. As great as these products are, only Steve Jobs could have captivated the audience the way he did, when he presented. Some tips from the book are to create a story, deliver the experience, and refine and rehearse.

Jobs always gave a story such as how he introduced the first Macintosh battling the corporate bully IBM. He delivered an experience when giving presentations by eliminating bullet points and clutter in favor of pictures that got the message across. As the adage goes, a picture is worth a thousand words. Finally, he practiced for hours by himself. Spectators of his presentations remarked that every slide was perfectly timed and written like a piece of poetry. Jobs never failed to deliver. He had immense stage presence and made sure the audience saw him eye to eye on the greatness of his products.

To present like Steve Jobs is an imposing task. However you can do better by simply following some basic tips. Maintain eye contact with everyone in the room. Maintain good posture and pace comfortably around if the space allows. Speak with a strong voice that starts from your chest. Good body language and a strong voice however are not enough if you are not an expert on your product or topic. The next time you have a presentation, do not try your luck by winging it but rather adopt the basics and keep the techniques used by Jobs in mind.

- Key Vocabulary
- Idioms and Expressions

해석

훌륭한 발표

당신은 세계에서 제일 좋은 아이디어가 있다. 그러나 다른 사람에게 설명하지 못하고 설득하지 못한다면 그건 전혀 좋은 것이 아니다. 〈스티브 잡스의 프레젠테이션 비밀〉이라는 책에서는 스티브 잡스처럼 발표하는 방법에 관한 몇 가지 조언들이 있다. 그의 APPLE에서의 재임기간 동안 잡스는 아이폰, 아이팟 그리고 아이패드를 소개했다. 이 제품들은 완전히 새로운 제품 카테고리를 시작하게 만들었고 경쟁자들은 그 행보에 참여하기 위해 앞다투어 몰려들었다. 이런 제품들이 훌륭할수록 오직 스티브 잡스만이 그가 발표를 할 때 했던 방법으로 청중들의 마음을 사로잡을 수 있었다. 이 책에 있는 팁들은 이야기를 만들기 위해, 경험 전달을 위해 그리고 개선과 연습을 위한 것들이다.
잡스는 그가 깡패 기업 IBM과 맞붙어 어떻게 첫 매킨토시를 소개했는지와 같은 이야기를 항상 했다. 그는 프레젠테이션을 할 때 중요 항목 표시들은 제거하고 메시지가 전달되는 많은 사진들을 채워 넣으며 경험을 전달한다. '천 마디 말보다 한번 보는 게 낫다'는 속담처럼. 마지막으로, 그는 몇 시간이고 혼자 연습했다. 잡스의 발표회 관중들은 모든 슬라이드는 완벽하게 시간이 맞게 설정되었고 한 편의 시처럼 쓰여 있었다고 말했다. 잡스는 전달하는데 절대 실패하지 않았다. 그는 청중을 휘어잡는 강한 힘이 있었고 그의 훌륭한 제품들에 대해 청중들의 의견이 자신(잡스)과 일치하도록 확실히 했다.
스티브 잡스처럼 발표하는 것은 인상적인 일이다. 그러나 몇몇 기본적인 조언들을 따르면 당신이 더 잘할 수 있다. 방에 있는 모두에게 지속적으로 눈을 맞춰라. 바른 자세를 유지하고 공간에 여유가 있다면 편하게 서성거려라. 당신의 가슴에서 시작하는 큰 목소리로 말해라. 당신이 만약 당신의 제품이나 주제에 대해 전문가가 아니라면 좋은 몸짓 언어와 큰 목소리는 충분하지 않다. 다음에 당신이 프레젠테이션을 한다면, 임기응변으로 되든 안되든 한번 해보지 말고 (발표의) 기초적인 방식을 택하고 잡스가 사용한 방법들을 명심해라.

Unit 09. Presenting Well

Key Vocabulary and Phrases

1. Persuade
2. Tenure
3. Category
4. Scrambling
5. Captivate
6. Deliver
7. Refine
8. Rehearse
9. Bully
10. Eliminate
11. Clutter
12. Adage
13. Spectator
14. Immense
15. Presence
16. Imposing
17. Adopt
18. To get in on the action
19. Getting the message across
20. Never failing to deliver
21. Winging it

Idioms and Expressions

1. A picture is worth a thousand words
2. Seeing eye to eye
3. Trying your luck

Unit 09. Presenting Well

Fill in the blanks with the appropriate word

1. The old ___________ that says the early bird gets the worm seems true.

2. Clear the _______________ in your office to feel more organized.

3. Carlos Slim has an _____________ fortune.

4. She had a ______________ taste in music.

5. Apple started a whole new product ________________ with the IPad.

Match the word with the one that shows its opposite meaning

1. Bully	**a)** Unimpressive
2. Imposing	**b)** Dissuade
3. Adopt	**c)** Renounce
4. Captivate	**d)** Nerd
5. Persuade	**e)** Discard

Conversation Questions

1. What are the key tips in making a great presentation?
2. What made Steve Jobs a good presenter?
3. Discuss your best and worst presentations ever.
4. What is the best presentation you have ever heard?
5. How can you improve your presentation skills?
6. Why do some people feel so nervous about giving presentations?
7. Whose presentation would you like to see in the world and why?
8. Describe your top three favorite public speakers. Why do you like them?
9. How is the body language different between Koreans and foreigners?

Assignment

Write a sentence using each of the key vocabulary word and idiom given above.

Vocabulary

1. ______________________________
2. ______________________________
3. ______________________________
4. ______________________________
5. ______________________________

6.

7.

8.

9.

10.

11.

12.

13.

14.

15.

16.

17.

18.

19.

20.

21.

22.

Idioms

1.

2.

3.

Class Idea

Give a presentation on your favorite book or film. Discuss the characters, setting, and the plot. Then explain how the story relates to your personal life.

Explore Further

On YouTube listen to the TED talk

Nancy Duarte Uncovers Common Structure of Greatest Communicators

Definition of Key Words

- **Tenure** n. — the amount of time that a person holds a job or office;
  the right to keep a job; the right to use property; *He became a tenured professor.*
  Synonyms: hitch, stint, term, tour
  Origin: Middle English, from Anglo-French, first known use in the 15th century

- **Captivate** v. — to attract and hold the attention of someone by being interesting, pretty, etc.
  The play has been captivating audiences for years.
  Synonyms: allure, beguile, bewitch, charm, enchant, magnetize
  Origin: first known use in 1555

Unit 09. Presenting Well

- **Scramble** v. to move or climb over something quickly, to move or act quickly; to prepare eggs by mixing the white and yellow parts together; *Both players scrambled for the ball.*
  Synonyms: clamber, scrabble, climb, swarm
  Origin: first known use in 1568

- **Refine** v. to remove the unwanted substances in something;
  to improve something by making small changes;
  The class is meant to help you refine your writing style.
  Synonyms: enhance, enrich, perfect, improve, upgrade
  Origin: first known use in 1582

- **Rehearse** v. to prepare for a public performance of a play, to say or do something several times in order to practice; *The lawyers rehearsed their closing arguments.*
  Synonyms: exercise, practice, run over
  Origin: Middle English, from Anglo-French, first known use in the 14th century

- **Bully** v. to frighten, hurt, or threaten;
  to cause someone to do something by making threats or insults or by using force;
  He bullied his younger brothers.
  Synonyms: brutalize, abuse, ill-treat, manhandle, mishandle, misuse
  Origin: French, first known use in 1753

- **Eliminate** v. to remove something that is not wanted or needed;
  to defeat and remove from a competition;
  The body naturally eliminates waste products.
  Synonyms: ban, close out, debar, exclude, shut out
  Origin: Latin, first known use in 1568

- **Clutter** v. to fill or cover something with many things;
  to fill or cover something with clutter;
  The garage was cluttered with tools.

- **Clutter** n. a large amount of things that are not arranged in a neat or orderly way;
  a crowded or disordered collection of things;
  There's a lot of unnecessary clutter in the house.
  Synonyms: agglomerate, mishmash, mélange, collage, hodgepodge
  Origin: first known use in 1649

- **Adage** n. an old and well-known saying that expresses a general truth;
  That old adage says "the early bird gets the worm."
  Synonyms: aphorism, maxim, proverb, saying
  Origin: Middle French, from Latin, first known use in 1513

- **Spectator** n. a person who watches an event, show, game, activity, etc. often as part of an audience;
  The accident attracted a large crowd of spectators.
  Synonyms: bystander, observer, onlooker, viewer, watcher
  Origin: Latin, first known use in 1586

- **Immense** adj. very great in size or amount;
  He inherited an immense fortune.
  Synonyms: imposing, astronomical, colossal, enormous, mega, whopping
  Origin: Middle English, from Middle French, first known use in the 15th century

- **Adopt** v. to take a child of other parents legally as your own child; to begin to use or have a different manner, method, etc.; to begin to use;
  He was adopted as an infant.
  Synonyms: borrow, embrace, espouse, take on, take up
  Origin: Middle English, from Middle French, first known use in 1500

pp. 99~101 한국어 해설

훌륭한 발표

주요단어 및 구절

1. 설득하다
2. 재임기간
3. 분류
4. 서둘러, 무질서한
5. 마음을 사로잡다
6. 전달하다
7. 개선하다
8. 예행연습(하다)
9. 깡패
10. 제거하다
11. 채우다, 잡동사니
12. 속담
13. 관중
14. 엄청난
15. 존재, 있음, 현장감
16. 인상적인
17. 받아들이다, 택하다
18. 편승하다, 끼어들다
19. 메시지를 전달하는
20. 전달하는데 절대 실패하지 않다
21. 임기응변하다

숙어 및 표현

1. 천마디 말보다 한번 보는 게 낫다
2. 의견이 일치하는[기]
3. 되든 안 되든 한번 해보는[기]

빈칸 채우기

1. Adage
2. Clutter
3. Immense
4. Refined
5. Category

반대의 의미 단어 찾기

1. d
2. e
3. c
4. a
5. b

대화 질문

1. 훌륭한 프레젠테이션을 하는 중요한 팁은 무엇인가?
2. 무엇이 스티븐 잡스를 좋은 발표자로 만들었는가?
3. 너의 최고, 최악의 발표를 논해보아라.
4. 당신이 여태까지 들었던 최고의 프레젠테이션은 무엇인가?
5. 어떻게 하면 프레젠테이션기술을 향상시킬 수 있는가?
6. 왜 어떤 사람들은 프레젠테이션하는 것에 대해 매우 긴장하는가?
7. 너는 세상에서 누구의 프레젠테이션을 보고 싶은가? 이유는?
8. 당신이 좋아하는 최고 공개 연설가 3명을 묘사해보아라. 왜 그들을 좋아하는가?
9. 한국인들과 외국인들 사이 몸짓언어는 어떻게 다른가?

과제

위에 주어진 단어와 숙어를 가지고 문장을 만드시오.

수업 아이디어

당신이 좋아하는 책이나 영화에 대한 프레젠테이션을 하라. 등장인물, 배경 그리고 구조를 논하여 보아라. 그리고 이 이야기가 어떻게 당신의 삶에 관계되는지 설명하여라.

Unit 10

Beating Procrastination

Today, here, now you might be thinking. Despite the to-do lists and goals you have made, you just cannot get everything done. In reality, most of us are very good at procrastination. We put off doing something until the last minute. Friends call about the favor they asked you and you apologize and say you dropped the ball. If we can just think straight and stop procrastinating, we might actually get all of our work done.

Avoiding procrastination is easier said than done. Based on the pleasure principle, we are hardwired to avoid negative emotions and delay stressful tasks. That means instead of doing our homework or working on our project, we instead play Nintendo or watch another rerun on TV. In the short term, we get some gratification and delay our responsibilities, which lead to further stress in the end, creating a significant negative feedback loop into doing less, worrying about doing more, and doing less. Students especially suffer from procrastination. Student syndrome is a phenomenon where students exert themselves right before a deadline. This sort of cramming is bad for retaining memory over the long term so it is crucial to beat procrastination and establish better habits to get work done.

Here are some tips on beating procrastination: Instead of having an infinite to-do list, create a realistic weekly to-do list. From your weekly to-do list, create a daily list that prioritizes your most important tasks. Then during your day, just focus on completing your daily to-do list. In this way, you will knock off the important things to do first. Remember to ignore everything else on the weekly list after you finish your daily list. This creates a positive feedback loop from feeling satisfied over completing your daily tasks while having your whole week already planned out in advance. This is a simple method based on reducing stress to accomplish more.

Do heed the Pareto principle or otherwise known as the 80–20 rule. About 80% of your productivity will come from 20% of your time. Or for those in business, 80% of your sales will come from 20% of your clients. Therefore, the name-of-the-game is to make sure you plan your important tasks when you are most alert and ready to get work done. The bottom line is to find a method that works for you, so that you reach your goals faster.

• Key Vocabulary
• Idioms and Expressions

해석

미루기 극복하기

오늘날 여기에서, 당신은 생각할지도 모른다. 당신이 만든 해야 할 일의 목록이나 목표들에도 불구하고 넌 모든 것을 마치지 못할 수 있다. 사실 우리 모두가 미루기를 잘한다. 우린 마지막까지 항상 미룬다. 친구들이 너에게 부탁했던 일에 대하여 전화하면 넌 그냥 일을 망쳤다고 하며 사과를 한다. 만약 우리가 논리적으로 생각하고 미루지 않는다면 우린 아마 모든 일을 끝낼 수 있을 것이다.

미루는 것을 피한다는 것은 말이야 쉽다. 쾌락 원칙에 따라 우리는 부정적 감정을 피하고 스트레스 받는 일을 미루도록 타고났다. 이 말은 숙제나 프로젝트를 하는 대신 닌텐도를 하거나 TV 재방송을 본다는 뜻이다. 단기에는 우린 만족감을 얻고 결국 더 스트레스를 주는 책임을 미루고, 일을 덜하고, 일을 하는 것을 더 많이 걱정하고, 일을 덜하는 명백히 부정적인 피드백 순환을 만든다. 특히 학생들은 미루기로 고통받는다. 학생 증후군이란 마감시간 바로 직전에만 주력하는 현상을 말한다. 이런 종류의 벼락치기는 기억을 장기간 유지하는데 나쁘다. 그래서 미루는 버릇을 없애고 일을 끝내는 더 나은 습관을 기르는 것은 중요하다.

여기 미루기를 이겨 내는 몇 가지 조언이 있다 : 끝없는 해야 할 일 목록을 가지고 있는 것보다 주 중에 해야 할 현실적인 목록을 만들어라. 주 중 할 일 목록에서 너의 제일 중요한 일의 우선순위가 있는 일일 할 일 목록을 만들어라. 그리고 하루 중에 그저 일일 할 일 목록을 끝내는 것에 집중하라. 이 방법으로, 너는 첫 번째 해야 할 중요한 일들을 끝낼 것이다. 당신이 매일 할 일 목록을 마친 뒤 다른 모든 주 중 할 일 목록을 무시하는 것을 기억해라. 이것은 너의 한 주가 이미 면밀이 계획되는 동안에 당신이 매일 할 일을 마쳤다는 만족감으로부터 긍정적인 피드백 순환을 만든다. 이것은 보다 더 많은 것을 성취하기 위해 스트레스를 줄인다는 데 근거한 단순한 방법이다.

파레토 원칙 혹은 80–20법칙이라고도 알려져 있는 것에 귀 기울여라. 너의 약 80% 생산성은 20%의 시간에서 나올 것이다. 또는 비즈니스에서는 80%의 매출은 20%의 고객으로부터 나온다는 말이다. 그러므로 가장 중요한 것은 당신이 가장 초롱초롱하고 일을 끝낼 준비가 되었을 때 중요한 일들을 계획하는 것이다. 핵심은 너에게 맞는 방법을 찾는 것이다. 그래서 너의 목표에 빠르게 다가가는 것이다.

Unit 10. Beating Procrastination

Key Vocabulary and Phrases

1. Favor
2. Hardwired
3. Delay
4. Rerun
5. Gratification
6. Phenomenon
7. Exert
8. Deadline
9. Cramming
10. Retain
11. Crucial
12. Procrastination
13. Infinite
14. To-do list
15. Heed
16. Put off until the last minute
17. Feedback loop
18. Student syndrome
19. 80–20 rule
20. Prioritize
21. Alert
22. Until the last minute

Idioms and Expressions

1. Think straight
2. The name-of-the-game
3. The bottom line

Fill in the blanks with the appropriate word

1. It is ________________ to drink enough water every day.

2. Traveling can always be new because there are ____________ places to visit and see.

3. The ______________ for my homework is tomorrow.

4. I will ___________ my parents if I can get a great job after graduation.

5. Lions are ____________ to hunt.

Match the word with the one that shows its opposite meaning

1. Delay	**a)** Hurry
2. Favor	**b)** Scatter
3. Infinite	**c)** Disrespect
4. Alert	**d)** Countable
5. Prioritize	**e)** Incautious

Explore Further

On YouTube listen to the TED talk by Vik Nithy

Why we procrastinate

Unit 10. Beating Procrastination

Conversation Questions

1. Why do people procrastinate?
2. Do you consider yourself a procrastinator?
3. Who is the greatest procrastinator that you know?
4. How can we beat procrastination?
5. What important things are you delaying now?
6. Are there some things you wanted to do but really need to let go?
7. Would you rather be busy and accomplish more or be stress-free and take it easy?
8. Are some cultures more rushed or relaxed in terms of getting things done?
9. What is the difference between patience and procrastination?
10. What positive and negative feedback loops do you have in your life?

Assignment

Write a sentence using each of the vocabulary and idiom given above.

Vocabulary

1. ______________________________
2. ______________________________
3. ______________________________
4. ______________________________
5. ______________________________
6. ______________________________

7.

8.

9.

10.

11.

12.

13.

14.

15.

16.

17.

18.

19.

20.

21.

22.

Idioms

1.

2.

3.

Unit 10. Beating Procrastination

Definition of Key Words

• **Delay** n. a situation in which something happens later than it should;
the amount of time that you must wait for something that is late;
What's causing the delay?

• **Delay** v. to wait until later to do something; to make something take longer than expected or planned;
He's planning to delay his retirement.
Synonyms: detention, holdback, holdup, wait
Origin: first known use in the 13th century

• **Rerun** v. to show a television program again; to do or run something again;
He reran the software on my computer.
Origin: first known use in 1934

• **Gratified** v. to make someone happy or satisfied;
to do or have whatever is wanted or demanded by someone or something;
A guilty verdict would gratify the victim's relatives.
Synonyms: cater, indulge, humor
Origin: Middle French, first known use in 1539

• **Phenomenon** n. something that can be observed and studied and that typically is unusual or difficult to understand or explain fully;
someone or something that is very impressive or popular especially because of an unusual ability or quality;
The movie eventually became a cultural phenomenon.
Synonyms: flash, marvel, miracle, wonder, sensation
Origin: Late Latin, from Greek, first known use in 1605

• **Deadline** n. a date or time when something must be finished;
We had to hurry to meet the deadline.
Origin: first known use in 1864

• **Cram** v. to fill something so that there is no room for anything else;
to push or force into a space that is tight or crowded;
He crammed the suitcase with his clothes.
Synonyms: crowd, crush, jam, squeeze, wedge
Origin: Middle English, from Old English, first known use in the 12th century

• **Retain** v. to continue to have or use something; to keep someone in a position, job, etc.;
You may need to retain an attorney.
Synonyms: hold, reserve, keep, withhold
Origin: Middle English, from Anglo-French, first known use in the 15th century

• **Crucial** adj. extremely important;
Vitamins are crucial for maintaining good health.
Synonyms: critical, key, pivotal, vital
Origin: French, from Latin, first known use in 1706

• **Procrastinate** v. to be slow or late about doing something that should be done;
to delay something until a later time because you do not want to do it;
He told her to stop procrastinating and get to work.
Origin: Latin, first known use in 1588

• **Infinite** adj. having no limits; extremely large or great;
There seemed to be an infinite number of possibilities.
Synonyms: bottomless, boundless, endless, unlimited, measureless
Origin: Middle English, from Anglo-French, first known use in the 14th century

• **Prioritize** v. to organize things so that the most important thing is done or dealt with first;
to make something the most important thing in a group;
It's always difficult to prioritize work, school, and family.
Origin: first known use in 1961

• **Alert** adj. able to think clearly and to notice things;
An alert guard stopped the robbers.
Synonyms: attentive, awake, observant, open-eyed, vigilant
Origin: first known use in 1618

pp. 110~113 한국어 해설

꾸물거림 극복하기

주요단어 및 구절

1. 부탁
2. 타고난, 선천적인
3. 지연, 연기하다
4. 재방송
5. 희열, 만족감
6. 현상
7. 노력하다, 분투하다
8. 마감기한
9. 벼락치기
10. 유지하다
11. 중요한
12. 연기, 지연, 꾸물거림
13. 무한의, 끝없는
14. 해야 할 일 목록
15. 주의를 기울이다
16. 마지막 순간까지 미루다
17. 피드백 순환
18. 학생 증후군
19. 80-20 법칙
(이탈리아 경제학자 파레토의 원리라고 불리는 법칙
20%의 이탈리아 국민들이 국부의 80%를 차지하고 있다)
20. 우선순위를 매기다
21. 초롱초롱한, 생기 있는
22. 마지막 순간까지

숙어 및 표현

1. 논리적으로 생각하다
2. 가장 중요한 것
3. 핵심은, 요점은

빈칸 채우기

1. Crucial
2. Infinite
3. Deadline
4. Gratify
5. Hardwired

반대의 의미 단어 찾기

1. a
2. c
3. d
4. e
5. b

대화 질문

1. 왜 사람들은 미루는가?
2. 당신 자신을 미루는 사람으로 보는가?
3. 당신이 아는 가장 많이 미루는 사람은 누구인가?
4. 우리는 어떻게 미루기를 극복할 수 있는가?
5. 당신이 지금 미루고 있는 중요한 것들은 무엇인가?
6. 당신이 하고 싶지만 정말 내버려 둬야 하는 것들이 있는가?
7. 당신은 바쁘고 더 성취하겠는가 아니면 차라리 스트레스 받지 않고 쉬엄쉬엄하겠는가?
8. 일을 마치는 면에서 더 서두르거나 더 느긋한 문화들이 있는가?
9. 참을성과 미루기 사이의 차이점은 무엇인가?
10. 당신의 삶에서 당신이 가진 긍정적 피드백 순환과 부정적 피드백 순환은 무엇인가?

과제

위에 주어진 단어와 숙어를 가지고 문장을 만드시오.

Unit 11

Great Leadership

John Maxwell said "A leader is one who knows the way, goes the way, and shows the way." Peter Drucker distinguished management from leadership and said "Management is doing things right; Leadership is doing the right things." These quotes help us understand what leadership is about but it is easier said than done. Certainly leaders want the respect and admiration of followers. But no one will follow if the leader does not have character. True leadership or respect is earned, not demanded. If you lack the morals to be a person worthy of respect, in the long run, you will lose the faith of others.

Some traits of leadership are resilience, positive energy, and passion. Leaders need resilience because they are the subject of criticism when things go wrong or the envy of others when things go right. Through tough times, leaders need to bounce back, admit mistakes, and communicate well with employees. They need resilience because they have to stay on top of all the responsibilities that a leader has.

Leaders must also display a go-getter attitude and give out positive energy. There are a multitude of benefits to being positive, such as thinking in terms of solutions and not problems, or being more open to risk taking and innovation. In every company, there will be negative people or some basket case who try to ruin the vibe of the organizational culture but a positive leader can be an example for others to rally behind and follow.

Passion is another trait reguired by leaders. Across the board, people are drawn to those with passion. A passionate person is evident to others because of his/her authentic excitement about the work. Passion is infectious and others will get the message to work in an enthusiastic way. Ultimately, actions speak louder than words, so it is important that leaders manifest resilience, positive energy, and passion on a consistent basis. Now knowing what is expected of leaders, are you ready to lead?

- Key Vocabulary
- Idioms and Expressions

해석

훌륭한 리더십

존 맥스웰은 "리더는 자기가 가는 길을 알고 그 길을 가고 또한 그 길을 보여줄 수 있는 사람이다."라고 말했다. 피터 드러커는 리더십과 경영을 구별했다. 그리고 "경영은 일을 올바르게 하는 것이고 리더십은 올바른 일을 하는 것이다."라고 말했다. 이런 인용문들은 리더십이 무엇에 관한 건지 이해를 도와준다. 하지만 말은 쉽지만 행동하기는 어렵다. 분명히 리더는 추종자들의 존경과 감탄을 원한다. 그러나 리더가 성품이 없다면 아무도 따르지 않을 것이다. 진정한 리더십과 존경은 얻어지는 것이지 요구하는 것이 아니다. 당신이 존경받을 만한 사람이 아니라면 장기적으로는 사람들에게 신임을 잃을 것이다.

리더십의 특성은 회복력, 긍정적인 힘 그리고 열정이다. 리더는 일이 잘못될 때에는 비판의 대상이 되거나 일이 잘 될 때는 질투의 대상이 되므로 회복력이 필요하다. 힘든 시간을 통하여 리더들은 회복하고 잘못을 인정하며 직원들과 소통을 잘 해야 한다. 그들은 리더이기에 수반되는 모든 일의 책임을 잘 해내야 하기 때문에 회복력이 필요하다.

리더는 또한 성공하려고 굳게 결심한 태도를 보여 주어야 하고 긍정적인 에너지를 발산해야 한다. 긍정적인 사람이 되는 것은 문제가 아니라 해결이라는 측면에서 생각하기 또는 위험 감수 그리고 혁신에 더 개방적 일 수 있는 것 같은 많은 이익들이 있다. 모든 회사에는, 조직문화 분위기를 망치려는 부정적인 사람들이나 머리가 이상한 사람들이 있다. 그러나 긍정적인 리더는 사람들이 (자기를) 지지하고 따르도록 모범이 될 수 있다.

열정은 리더가 필요로 하는 또 하나의 특징이다. 전반적으로 사람들은 열정이 있는 사람에게 끌린다. 열정적인 사람은 다른 사람들의 눈에 띈다. 왜냐하면 열정적인 사람은 자신의 일을 신나하는 것이 진짜이기 때문이다. 열정은 전염성이 있기에 다른 사람들도 알아채고 열심히 일한다. 결국 말보다 행동이 중요하다. 그래서 리더들이 회복력, 긍정적 에너지 그리고 열정을 계속 나타내는 것이 중요하다. 이제 리더에게 무엇을 기대하는지 알았으니, 이끌 준비가 되어 있는가?

Unit 11. Great Leadership

Key Vocabulary and Phrases

1. Distinguished
2. Management
3. Admiration
4. Character
5. Leadership
6. Respect
7. In the long run
8. Faith
9. Resilience
10. Positive energy
11. Passion
12. Envy
13. Go-getter
14. Multitude
15. Solution
16. Innovation
17. Vibe
18. Rally behind
19. Evident
20. Enthusiastic
21. Ultimately
22. Manifest
23. Consistent

Idioms and Expressions

1. Easier said than done
2. Stay on top of things
3. Basket case
4. Across the board
5. Actions speak louder than words

Unit 11. Great Leadership

Fill in the blanks with the appropriate word

1. Great ___________ means taking care of the people that need you.

2. _____________ is essential to being a devout Muslim.

3. He was always ____________ about exercising and eating well so he looks many years younger than his biological age.

4. I am so ______________ about going on vacation to Paris this winter break!

5. When there is a problem, leaders have a _________________.

Match the word with the one that shows its opposite meaning

1. Faith	**a)** Doubt
2. Solution	**b)** Quandary
3. Multitude	**c)** Goodwill
4. Envy	**d)** Unyielding
5. Resilience	**e)** Handful

Conversation Starters

1. When you think of a leader, who comes first to mind? Describe their leadership style.
2. Why are passion and positive energy important for a leader?
3. What is the hardest part of being a leader?
4. Who are some of the greatest leaders in your country from business, politics, or sports? Discuss their achievements and leadership style.
5. Is it okay to question the order of leaders or should you simply follow?
6. Should you respect people just because of their higher position or do they first need to earn your respect? If so, how can you earn it?
7. As a leader of your school or company, what changes would you make?
8. As a president of your country, what changes would you make?
9. Who are some of the worst leaders throughout world history?
10. What characteristics do all leaders possess?
11. What can you do to grow and develop as a leader?
12. Describe someone who has had a tremendous impact on your life. How did they influence you?

Explore Further

On YouTube listen to the TED talk by John Wooden

The Difference between Winning and Succeeding

Unit 11. Great Leadership

Assignment

Write a sentence using each of the vocabulary and idiom given above.

Vocabulary

1.

2.

3.

4.

5.

6.

7.

8.

9.

10.

11.

12.

13.

14.

15.

16.

17.

18.

19.

20.

21.

22.

23.

Idioms

1.

2.

3.

4.

5.

Definition of Key Words

• **Distinguished** adj. known by many people because of some quality or achievement; making someone seem important and worth respect; *She is distinguished for her achievements in genetic research.*
Synonyms: dignified, imposing, portly, solemn, stately
Origin: first known use in 1714

• **Admiration** n. a feeling of great respect and approval; *She looked at them in admiration.*
Synonyms: account, appreciation, esteem, favor, regard, respect
Origin: first known use in the 15th century

Unit 11. Great Leadership

- **Character** n. — the way someone thinks, feels, and behaves; someone's personality;
  a set of qualities that are shared by many people in a group, country, etc.;
  Their house has a lot of character.
  Synonyms: sign, symbol, icon, disposition
  Origin: Middle English, from Latin, first known use in the 14th century

- **Respect** n. — a feeling of admiring someone or something that is good, valuable, important, etc.;
  a particular way of thinking about or looking at someone;
  He has earned their respect.

- **Respect** v. — to feel admiration for someone or something;
  to act in a way that shows that you are aware of someone's rights, wishes, etc.
  Synonyms: reference, regard
  Origin: first known use in 1560

- **Faith** n. — strong belief or trust in someone or something;
  belief in the existence of God; a system of religious beliefs;
  Nothing is more important to her than her faith in God.
  Synonyms: devotion, piety, religion
  Origin: Middle English, from Anglo-French, first known use in the 13th century

- **Resilience** n. — the ability to become strong, healthy, or successful again after something bad happens;
  the ability of something to return to its original shape after it has been pulled, stretched, pressed, bent, etc.;
  He showed remarkable resilience in dealing with a difficult childhood.
  Origin: first known use in 1824

- **Go-getter** n. — a person who works very hard and who wants very much to succeed;
  He was always a go-getter so I could see why he became rich.
  Synonyms: self-starter, hustler, highflyer
  Origin: first known use in 1919

- **Innovation** n. — a new idea, device, or method especially for commercialization;
  He is responsible for many innovations in his field.
  Synonyms: concoction, creation, invention, brainchild
  Origin: first known use in the 15th century

- **Vibe** n. a feeling that someone or something gives you;
  I got a weird vibe from her.
  Synonyms: aura, chi, vibe, vibration
  Origin: first known use in 1967

- **Evident** adj. clear to the sight or mind;
  The problems have been evident for quite some time.
  Synonyms: apparent, ostensible, ostensive, presumed, reputed
  Origin: first known use in the 14th century

- **Enthusiastic** adj. feeling or showing strong excitement about something;
  filled with or marked by enthusiasm;
  She received an enthusiastic welcome.
  Synonyms: anxious, ardent, crazy, eager, greedy
  Origin: first known use in 1603

- **Manifest** adj. able to be seen; clearly shown or visible;
  easy to understand or recognize;
  Their sadness was manifest in their faces.
  Synonyms: apparent, distinct, evident, lucid, obvious
  Origin: Middle English, from Anglo-French, first known use in the 14th century

- **Consistent** adj. always acting or behaving in the same way;
  of the same quality, good every time;
  happening in the same way;
  The decision was consistent with the company's policy.
  Synonyms: coherent, compatible, congruent, harmonious
  Origin: Latin, first known use in 1638

pp. 119~122 한국어 해설

훌륭한 리더십

주요단어 및 구절

1. 구별되는
2. 경영
3. 감탄, 존경
4. 성품, 개성
5. 리더십
6. 존경
7. 장기에는
8. 믿음, 신뢰
9. 회복력
10. 긍정적 에너지
11. 열정
12. 부러움
13. 성공하려고 단단히 작정한
14. 다수, 아주 많은
15. 해결책, 해답
16. 혁신
17. 분위기
18. 지지하다
19. 분명한, 눈에 띄는
20. 열렬한, 열심인
21. 결국, 궁극적으로, 근본적으로
22. 나타내다, 분명해지다
23. 한결같은, 일치하는

숙어 및 표현

1. 행동보다 말이 쉽다, 말이야 쉽다
2. 매사에 훤히 알다, 잘 하다
3. 마비된 것, 머리가 이상한 사람
4. 전반에 걸쳐서
5. 백문이 불여일견, 말보다 행동

빈칸 채우기

1. Leadership
2. Faith
3. Consistent
4. Enthusiastic
5. Solution

반대의 의미 단어 찾기

1. a
2. b
3. e
4. c
5. d

대화 시작 질문

1. 리더를 생각하면 누가 가장 먼저 떠오르는가? 그들의 리더십 스타일을 설명하라.
2. 왜 리더에게 열정과 긍정적 에너지가 중요한가?
3. 리더가 되는데 가장 힘든 부분은 무엇인가?
4. 당신의 나라에서 사업, 정치 혹은 스포츠에서 가장 훌륭한 리더들은 누구인가? 그들의 업적과 리더십 스타일을 설명하라.
5. 리더의 명령에 이의를 제기해도 되는가? 아니면 그냥 따라야 하는가?
6. 당신은 단지 높은 지위 때문에 누군가를 존경해야 하는가? 아니면 그들이 먼저 당신의 존경을 얻어야 하는가? 만약 그렇다면, 어떻게 얻을 수 있는가?
7. 당신이 학교나 회사의 리더라면, 어떤 변화를 만들 것인가?
8. 당신이 나라의 대통령이라면, 어떤 변화를 만들 것인가?
9. 세계 역사를 통틀어 최악의 리더는 누구인가?
10. 모든 리더들이 지니고 있는 성품은 무엇인가?
11. 리더로 자라고 발전하기 위해 무엇을 할 수 있는가?
12. 너의 인생에 엄청난 영향을 준 사람을 설명하라. 어떻게 영향을 주었나?

과제

위에 주어진 단어와 숙어를 사용해 문장을 만드시오.

Unit 12

Super Achievers

Successful people behave differently than unsuccessful people. Everybody wants to be successful or has a dream but is unwilling to pay the price. For example, we might want to be CEO but do not want the high stress and long hours required for the job. Or we want to be a lawyer but do not want the paralyzing debt of attending law school. However, beyond realizing that sacrifices have to be made and that you can't have your cake and eat it too is to learn a thing or two about the mindset that super achievers share.

First of all, these super achievers keep their eye on the ball. They realize that inevitable bumps will come along but are able to anticipate changes and embrace them as opportunities to learn and grow. They understand and accept that nothing is just a walk in the park. In addition, they take well-calculated risks. They understand that being too conservative or playing it safe will not lead to any huge home runs in life. They know the higher the risk, the greater the reward. Moreover, they trust their instincts. Anyone can think straight from the gut and be completely wrong, so they only

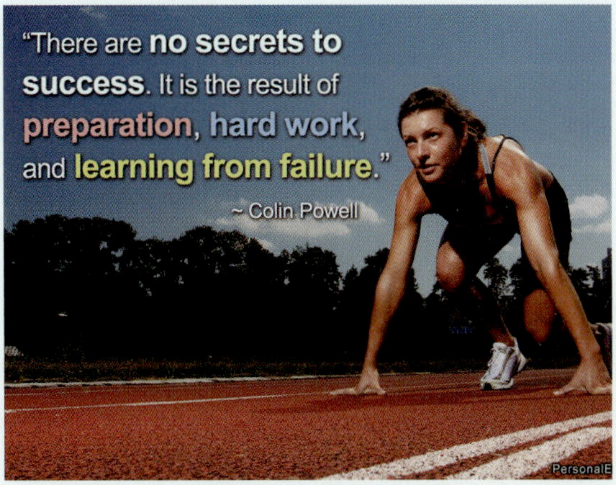

trust instinct when they have expertise in the situation. That is because humans are pattern-matching machines that compare previous experiences with similar situations and then store everything deep in their hidden or subconscious mind. To their benefit, they realize that intuition from experience is something completely different from a novice with a hunch.

Other differences highlight different lifestyles. Successful people read every day, keep a journal, give compliments, forgive others, and continuously learn. Unsuccessful people criticize others, never set goals, watch TV every day, and blame others for failures. On top of it, unsuccessful people feel sorry for themselves because they believe that life is not fair. Of course, these are just generalizations but you would be wise to learn a thing or two from the behaviors and lifestyles of successful people.

- Key Vocabulary
- Idioms and Expressions

해석

위대한 성공자들

성공한 사람들은 성공하지 못한 사람들과 다르게 행동한다. 모든 사람들이 성공을 원하거나 꿈이 있지만 대가를 치르기는 싫어한다. 예를 들어, 우리는 CEO가 되고 싶어 하지만 업무의 스트레스와 직장에 오래 남아 있어야 하는 것은 싫다. 혹은 우리는 변호사가 되고 싶어 하지만 로스쿨 학비의 끔찍한 빚은 원하지 않는다. 하지만 희생이 따라야만 하고 심지어 너는 케익을 먹고 또 가질 수는 없다(두 가지 다하는 것은 불가능하다 한 가지는 포기해야 함)는 깨달음 뒤에 한 두 개 성취도가 매우 높은 사람들의 사고방식을 배우는 것이다.
첫 번째로, 이러한 성취도가 매우 높은 사람들은 계속 주의를 기울인다. 그들은 피할 수 없는 방지 턱이 생기는 것을 알지만 변화를 예측할 수 있고 그런 방지 턱을 배우고 성장하는 기회로 수용할 수 있다. 그들은 어떠한 것도 쉬운 게 아니라는 것을 이해하고 받아들인다. 또한 그들은 면밀히 계획된 위험도 감수한다. 그들은 너무 보수적이거나 안전을 기하는 것은 인생에 큰 성공을 가져오지 않음을 이해한다. 그들은 위험이 클수록 보상도 더 크다는 것을 알고 있다. 더 나아가 그들은 그들의 직감을 믿는다. 누구든지 직감으로만 생각해서 완전히 틀릴 수 있기 때문에 그들은 그 상황의 전문지식이 있을 때에만 직감을 믿는다. 인간은 이전의 경험과 유사한 상황을 비교한 다음 숨어있는 의식 또는 잠재의식 깊은 곳에 모든 것을 저장하는 패턴 맞추기 기계이기 때문이다. 그들에게 이롭게도, 그들은 경험에서 나온 직감은 초보자의 감과는 완전히 다른 것임을 인식하고 있다.
다른 차이점들이 다른 생활방식을 강조한다. 성공한 사람들은 매일 읽고, 일기를 쓰고, 칭찬을 하고, 다른 이를 용서하고 그리고 계속해서 배운다. 성공하지 못한 사람들은 남을 비판하고, 목표를 절대 설정하지 않고, TV를 매일 보며 실패한 것에 대하여 남을 원망한다. 거기에다가, 성공하지 못한 사람들은 자신의 삶이 공정하지 않다고 믿기 때문에 한탄한다. 당연히, 이것들은 단지 일반화된 것이지만 당신은 성공한 사람들의 생활방식과 행동에서 한두 개 정도는 배울 만큼 현명할 것이라고 본다.

Unit 12. Super Achievers

Key Vocabulary and Phrases

1. Paralyzing
2. Debt
3. Sacrifice
4. Inevitable bumps
5. Anticipate
6. Well-calculated risks
7. Conservative
8. Reward
9. Instinct
10. Novice
11. Pattern-matching machines
12. Store
13. Subconscious
14. Intuition
15. Highlight
16. Feeling sorry for yourself
17. Fair
18. Generalization
19. Hunch

Idioms and Expressions

1. You can't have your cake and eat it too.
2. Keeping the eye on the ball
3. Playing it safe
4. Straight from the gut
5. On top of it all
6. Pay the price
7. A walk in the park

Unit 12. Super Achievers

Fill in the blanks with the appropriate word

1. Some people trust their __________ more than their logic.
2. A mother's __________ is to protect her child at all costs.
3. Any _________ basketball player can improve by focusing on the basics.
4. Financial stress from __________ can cause depression.
5. I have an ____________ that it will rain tomorrow.

Match the word with the one that shows its opposite meaning

1. Novice	**a)** Proof
2. Anticipate	**b)** Master
3. Hunch	**c)** Specific
4. Fair	**d)** Be unready
5. Generalization	**e)** Unjust

Explore Further

On YouTube listen to the TED talk by Richard St. John

The 8 Traits of Successful People

Conversation Starters

1. Describe a successful person.

2. Which friend do you consider the most successful and why?

3. How different are the habits and behaviors of successful people?

4. Of the three, what is the most important for success: looks, personality, or skill?

5. Make an all-inclusive definition for the word "success."

6. Can money buy happiness? Why or why not?

7. What failures have made your life better?

8. Where do you see yourself 10 years down the road?

9. If you were very rich, what would you do? How would you change?

10. Is your idea of success the same as your parents?

Assignment

Write a sentence using each of the key vocabulary word and idiom given above.

Vocabulary

1. ______________________________

2. ______________________________

3. ______________________________

4. ______________________________

5. ______________________________

6. ______________________________

7.

8.

9.

10.

11.

12.

13.

14.

15.

16.

17.

18.

19.

Idioms

1.

2.

3.

4.

5.

6.

7.

Class Idea

Interview a successful family member or someone who is working in your dream job and ask them the secrets to their success.

Definition of Key Words

- **Paralyze** v. to make a person unable to move or feel all or part of the body;
  The snake's venom paralyzed the mouse.
  Synonyms: cripple, disable, immobilize, incapacitate, prostrate
  Origin: French, first known use in 1804

- **Debt** n. an amount of money that you owe to a person;
  He is trying to pay off gambling debts.
  Synonyms: liability, obligation
  Origin: Middle English, first known use in the 13th century

- **Sacrifice** n. the act of giving up something that you want to keep especially in order to get or do something else or to help someone; a person or animal that is killed in a sacrifice;
  The war required everyone to make sacrifices.
  Synonyms: immolation, offering, victim
  Origin: Middle English, first known use in the 13th century

- **Anticipate** v. to think of something that will or might happen in the future;
  to expect or look ahead to with pleasure; to do something before someone else;
  The cost turned out to be higher than anticipated.
  Synonyms: expect, await, hope, watch
  Origin: Latin, first known use in 1532

- **Conservative** adj. believing in the value of established and traditional practices in politics and society;
  relating to or supporting political conservatism;
  She's more conservative now than she was in college.
  Synonyms: die-hard, old-school, old-fashioned, orthodox, traditional
  Origin: First known use in the 14th century

Unit 12. Super Achievers

- **Instinct** n. a way of behaving or thinking that is not learned; a natural desire that makes you want to act in a particular way; *Our first instinct was to run.*
  Origin: Middle English, from Latin, first known use in the 15th century

- **Novice** n. a person who has just started learning or doing something;
  a new member of a religious group who is preparing to become a nun or a monk;
  He's a novice in cooking.
  Synonyms: apprentice, fledgling, neophyte, newbie, recruit, rookie
  Origin: Middle English, from Anglo-French, first known use in the 14th century

- **Store** v. to put something in a place where it can be safely kept;
  to collect and put something into one location for future use; *She stores her jewels in a safe.*
  Synonyms: keep, put up, stow, hoard

- **Store** n. a building or room where things are sold; *I'm going to the store to buy groceries.*
  Origin: first known use in the 13th century

- **Subconscious** adj. existing in the part of the mind that a person is not aware of;
  existing in the mind but not consciously known or felt;
  Those feelings had been in her subconscious.
  Origin: first known use in 1834

- **Intuition** n. a natural ability or power that makes it possible to know something without any proof or evidence;
  a feeling that guides a person to act in a certain way without fully understanding why;
  something that is known or understood without proof or evidence;
  Intuition was telling her that something was very wrong.
  Origin: Middle English, from Late Latin, first known use in the 15th century

- **Fair** adj. agreeing with what is thought to be right or acceptable;
  treating people in a way that does not favor some over others; not too harsh or critical;
  That's a fair question, and it deserves an honest reply.
  Synonyms: impartial, unprejudiced, disinterested, neutral
  Origin: Middle English, from Old English, first known use in the 12th century

- **Hunch** n. an intuitive guess or feeling; a lump or large piece;
  My hunch tells me that the athlete cheated.
  Synonyms: surmise, feeling, conjecture
  Origin: first known use in 1590

pp. 129~133 한국어 해설

위대한 성공자들

주요단어 및 구절

1. 끔찍한
2. 빚, 부채
3. 희생
4. 피할 수 없는 방지 턱
5. 예상하다
6. 면밀이 계획된 위험
7. 보수적인
8. 보상
9. 직감, 본능
10. 초보자
11. 패턴 맞추기 기계
12. 저장하다
13. 잠재의식
14. 직관, 직관력, 직감
15. 강조하다
16. 한탄하다
17. 공평한, 타당한
18. 일반화
19. 예감, 감

숙어 및 표현

1. 케익을 먹고 또 가질 수는 없다 (두 마리 토끼를 동시에 잡을 수 없다; 한가지만 가능하다)
2. 주의를 기울이는[기], 방심하지 않는[기]
3. 안전을 기하다
4. 단지 직감으로
5. 게다가
6. 대가를 치르다
7. 쉬운

빈칸 채우기

1. Intuition
2. Instinct
3. Novice
4. Debt
5. Hunch

반대의 의미 단어 찾기

1. b
2. d
3. a
4. e
5. c

대화 시작 질문

1. 성공한 사람을 설명하시오.
2. 어떤 친구가 가장 성공했다고 생각하는가? 이유는?
3. 성공한 사람들의 습관과 행동은 어떻게 다른가?
4. 외모, 성격 그리고 재주 세 가지 중 성공에 가장 중요한 것은 무엇인가?
5. 성공이란 단어의 포괄적 정의를 내려라.
6. 돈으로 행복을 살 수 있는가? (그렇다면)이유는? (그러지 않다면)이유는?
7. 당신의 인생을 더 좋게 만든 실패는 무엇인가?
8. 10년 후 당신은 어떤 모습일 것 같은가?
9. 당신이 만약 엄청 부자라면, 무엇을 할 것인가? 어떻게 변할 것인가?
10. 당신의 성공에 대한 생각이 부모님의 생각과 같은가?

과제

위에 주어진 단어와 숙어를 가지고 문장을 만드시오.

수업 아이디어

성공한 가족 멤버나 당신이 희망하는 직업에서 일하는 사람을 면담해보고 그들의 성공비밀을 물어보시오.

03

Module 03.

Thinking beyond work 일 그 이상의 생각

Unit 13

Elite Colleges Worth It?

Every year in Korea, parents pray as their children take the soo-neung or the Korean SATs. On this day, even the police escort students so that they reach school on time. Students who fail to meet expectations, spare one or two extra years just for studying the exam again in the hopes of entering into a university in Seoul. In Korea, there is a perception that all roads lead to Seoul.

Entering into a Seoul university is a big deal because where you graduate from is believed to determine your career and sometimes even your marriage partner. Invariably despite family support and private tutoring, many students fall through the cracks. Some even fail to land back on their feet, believing that they have brought shame and humiliation to their families. But is where you spend that four years of your college life really that important? Are elite colleges worth the price tag?

Let us first discuss what an elite college or a world class university is. Some rankings exist such as the US News and World Report for American colleges, the QS World University Rankings from the U.K., and the Chosun Ilbo Rankings for Korean colleges. They take into account the research output of professors, intellectual ability as measured by standardized tests of students, and the reputation of the institution among other factors. Most elite universities around the world rank high and are the dream destinations of students all around the world.

About 80% of Korean high school students end up graduating from college. College life for some means a stable job but crippling debt from school loans often offsets the benefits. Many students after graduation enter into income-based repayment programs and especially for graduates of elite colleges with premium price tags one has to wonder if the experience was really worth the cost. Do elite colleges offer better connections or more earning potential or more successful careers?

In the U.S., the answers might surprise you. Google has stated that they disregard the university brand name. They realize talent comes in so many forms and look for people who can learn on the fly and think on their feet. They also look for those who have the right skills and not the credentials. Undoubtedly, some students are late bloomers or may not have worked hard in high school but have the natural talent to learn. Google's policy and HR system is to find talent existing everywhere and not just the talent that comes from the Ivy League.

Malcolm Gladwell in his book "David and Goliath" also mentioned about lesser known and elite schools. He suggests that students attend a lesser-known place over pursuing prestige at an elite school even if accepted. His reasoning is simple:

it is better to be a big fish in a small pond than a small fish in a big pond. If you are one of the best at your college and in your group, you are more likely to have the confidence and ability to truly stand out. He notes that at an elite institution, the very best will truly do great things leaving the rest feeling stupid and unsuccessful. Thus, the cream of the crop at lesser-known schools stay on the fast track, whereas the average and lower tier students at elite schools lag. His claims are striking and at the least it is something to chew on.

Further food for thought is that there is more variation within schools than between schools. For instance, the quality of the economics department at school no. 55 might be higher than the economics department at school no. 15. So before attending an elite university or having remorse for not attending one, one should have an open mind. Besides, accumulating knowledge does not always have to be about money or the job. Attaining knowledge can be just for the sake of knowledge.

- Key Vocabulary
- Idioms and Expressions

해석

명문대학 가치가 있는가?

매년 한국에서는, 아이들이 수능을 볼 때 부모들이 기도를 한다. 이날은 심지어 경찰도 그들이 학교에 제시간에 갈 수 있도록 호위한다. 시험 결과가 기대에 못 미치는 학생은 서울에 있는 대학에 입학하기를 바라며 다시 시험공부하는데 1~2년을 할애한다. 한국에서는 '모든 길은 서울로 통한다'라는 인식이 있다.

어떤 학교를 졸업하냐에 따라 직업과 심지어 결혼 상대까지 결정된다고 믿기 때문에 서울에 있는 대학교에 들어가는 것은 큰일이다. 가족의 지지 그리고 과외에도 불구하고 변함없이 많은 학생들은 (합격 명단에서) 빠져 있다. 몇몇은 심지어 가족들에게 부끄러움과 수치를 줬다고 믿으며 도전할 용기를 잃어버린다. 그러나 당신이 어느 곳에서 인생의 단지 4년을 보내는지가 정말 중요한가? 명문 대학이 가격표의 가치가 있는가?

첫 번째로 무엇이 명문 대학 혹은 세계적인 대학인지 토론해보자. 미국 대학을 위한 US 뉴스나 World Report, 영국의 QS 세계대학 순위 그리고 조선일보의 한국 대학 순위와 같은 몇몇의 순위표가 있다. 그들은 여러 요소들 중에서 교수들의 연구결과, 표준시험으로 측정된 학생들의 지적 능력 그리고 대학의 명성을 고려한다. 전 세계 대부분의 명문 대학들은 순위가 높으며 전 세계에 있는 학생들의 꿈의 목표이다.

한국 고등학생의 80%가 대학을 졸업한다. 어떤 이들에게 대학생활이란 안정된 직업을 갖는다는 의미이지만 이런 이익은 학자금 대출로 인한 주체할 수 없는 빚으로 상쇄된다. 많은 학생들은 졸업 후 소득 기준 상환 프로그램에 들어가며 특히 프리미엄 가격표를 단 명문 대학 졸업생들은 그 경험이 정말 가치가 있는지 의문이 마땅히 든다. 명문 대학이 더 나은 연줄, 더 많은 잠재 소득 혹은 더 성공적인 직업을 제공하는가?

미국에서의 답변들은 당신을 놀라게 할지도 모른다. 구글은 대학 이름은 무시한다고 명시했다. 그들은 재능은 여러 가지 형태라는 것을 깨닫고 그때 그때 배울 수 있고 빨리 대응을 할 수 있는 사람을 찾는다. 그들은 또한 증명서가 아닌 올바른 기술을 가진 사람을 찾고 있다. 의심할 여지 없이, 어떤 학생은 대기만성형이고 혹은 고등학생 때 공부를 열심히 하지는 않았지만 배우는데 있어서 천부적인 재능을 가진 사람도 있다. 구글의 정책과 인사 시스템은 아이비 리그에서 나오는 재능이 아닌 어디에서나 존재하는 재능을 찾는 것이다.

말콤 글래드웰의 책 〈다윗과 골리앗〉 또한 덜 유명한 학교에 관해 언급한다. 그는 학생들이 명문학교에 붙었다고 해도 덜 유명한 학교를 선택한다고 말했다. 그의 논리는 단순하다 : 큰 연못에서 작은 물고기가 되는 것보다는 작은 연못에서 큰 물고기가 되는 것이 낫다. 당신이 만약 당신의 대학에서나 무리에서 최고라면 당신은 진정으로 두드러지기 위해 자신감과 능력을 가질 가능성이 많다. 그는 명문 대학에서 최고 중의 최고는 정말 위대한 일을 하며 나머지들이 멍청하고 실패했다고 느끼게 한다고 기술했다. 따라서, 덜 유명한 학교에서 제일 우수한 학생들은 출세 가도(빠른 출세길)에 있는 반면 명문학교의 평균 그리고 이하의 층에 있는 학생들은 처진다. 그의 주장은 인상적이다. 그리고 최소한 생각을 해봐야 하는 것이다.

더 생각할 거리는 학교 간의 차이보다 학교 내의 차이가 더 많이 있다는 것이다. 예를 들어, 55번 경제학과의 질이 15번 경제학과 보다 더 높을 수 있다. 따라서 명문대에 들어가거나 들어가지 못한 것을 후회하기 전에, 열린 마음을 가져야 한다. 게다가 지식을 축적하는 것은 항상 돈이나 직업에 관련되지 않아도 된다. 지식을 얻는 것은 단지 지식 자체를 위해서일 수도 있다.

Unit 13. Elite Colleges Worth It?

Key Vocabulary and Phrases

1. SAT
2. Escort
3. Expectation
4. Big deal
5. Invariably
6. Shame
7. Humiliation
8. Elite
9. Ranking
10. Output
11. Stable
12. Offset
13. Crippling
14. Income-based repayment
15. Connection
16. Late bloomer
17. Policy
18. System
19. Prestige
20. Reasoning
21. Big fish in a small pond / Small fish in a big pond
22. Fast track
23. Lag
24. Striking
25. Accumulating
26. Knowledge for the sake of knowledge
27. Credential

Idioms and Expressions

1. Fall through the cracks
2. Land on your feet
3. Learn on the fly
4. Think on your feet
5. Cream of the crop
6. Food for thought
7. Something to chew on
8. All roads lead to Rome/Seoul

Fill in the blanks with the appropriate word

1. Russia's _________ controls most of the nation's wealth.

2. Many American law students face _____________ debt after graduation.

3. Some people pay premium price on luxury goods for the _____________.

4. Some Koreans think that a __________ career is better than a risky and high paying one.

5. Even people with all the right _____________ can be wrong on a subject in which they have no expertise.

Match the word with the one that shows its opposite meaning

1. Crippling	**a)** Input
2. Stable	**b)** Applaud
3. Output	**c)** Rickety
4. Elite	**d)** Commoners
5. Humiliate	**e)** Rehabilitate

Unit 13. Elite Colleges Worth It?

Conversation Questions

1. What are the top 10 universities in your country? What are their specialties?
2. Name top three universities in three different Asian countries.
3. What makes a university world class or elite?
4. Why is attending an elite university so important to many Koreans?
5. What is the difference between attending an elite school and a regular school?
6. Are elite schools worth the cost? Why or why not?
7. Do you agree with Gladwell's reasoning to attend a lesser known school?
8. Why did you choose your university and major?
9. What have you contributed to your university?
10. What have you learned the most from college life?

Explore Further

On YouTube listen to the TED talk by Malcolm Gladwell

The Unheard Story of David and Goliath

Assignment

Write a sentence using each of the key vocabulary word and idiom given above.

Vocabulary

1.

2.

3.

4.

5.

6.

7.

8.

9.

10.

11.

12.

13.

14.

15.

16.

17.

18.

19.

20.

21.

22.

23.

24.

25.

26.

27.

Idioms

1.

2.

3.

4.

5.

6.

7.

8.

Class Idea

Research the top three most widely used university rankings around the world. Compare the top 100 lists. What is interesting about your finding? Do you find anything surprising?

Definition of Key Words

- **Escort** n. — a person or group of people who go with someone to give protection guidance;
a group of vehicles, ships, or planes that provide protection;
a man who goes with a woman to a social event; *The bombers were protected by a fighter escort.*
Synonyms: attendant, companion, guard, guide
Origin: Middle French, from Italian, first known use in 1579

- **Invariably** adv. — on every occasion; always;
Their slacker son invariably gives the same response to the questions about his career plans.
Synonyms: consistently, constantly, incessantly, perpetually
Origin: first known use in 1646

- **Humiliate** v. — to make someone feel very ashamed or foolish;
I hope I don't humiliate myself during the presentation.
Synonyms: abase, cheapen, degrade, demean, dishonor
Origin: Latin, first known use in 1534

- **Elite** n. — the people who have the most wealth and status in a society;
a person who is a member of an elite; a successful and powerful person;
The country's elite controls most of the wealth.
Synonyms: aristocracy, best, choice, royalty, upper crust
Origin: French, first known use in 1823.

- **Output** n. — the amount of something that is produced by a person or thing;
something that is produced by a machine or system;
the place at which information, power, etc. comes out of a machine or system;
The computer's output is shown on this screen.
Synonyms: fruit, labor, product, produce, yield
Origin: first known use in 1858

- **Stable** n. — buildings in which horses are kept, fed, and cared for; *She rode the horse back to the stable.*

- **Stable** adj. — in a good state or condition that is not easily changed or likely to change;
They have a stable relationship.
Synonyms: fast, firm, sound, strong, sturdy
Origin: Middle English, from Anglo-French, first known use in the 13th century

Unit 13. Elite Colleges Worth It?

- **Offset** n.

something that sets to advantage or embellishes something else;
something that serves to counterbalance or to compensate for something else;
A better performance this time will be an offset to last year's dismal showing.
Synonyms: balance, corrective, counter, counterforce, counterbalance
Origin: first known use in 1555

- **Cripple** n.

a disabled person; something flawed or impact; *He returned from war a cripple.*

- **Cripple** v.

to cause a person or an animal to be unstable to move or walk normally;
The economy was crippled by inflation.
Origin: first known use in the 14th century

- **Prestige** n.

the respect and admiration that someone or something gets for being successful or important;
The job has low pay and low prestige.
Origin: French, from Middle French, first known use in 1829

- **Lag** v.

to stay or fall behind; to slacken or weaken gradually;
The runner lagged behind the leader for most of the race.
Synonyms: concluding, hindmost, last, latter, terminal
Origin: Scandinavian, first known use in 1514

- **Accumulate** v.

to gather or acquire something gradually as time passes;
to increases gradually in amount as time passes;
Evidence of his guilt is accumulating.
Synonyms: accelerate, increase, balloon, boom, escalate, proliferate
Origin: Latin, first known use in the 15th century

- **Credential** adj.

a quality, skill, or experience that makes a person suited to do a job;
a document which shows that a person is qualified to do a particular job;
My experience as a manager is my strongest credential.
Origin: first known use in 1888

pp. 142~146 한국어 해설

명문대학 가치가 있는가?

주요단어 및 구절

1. (미국)대학수능시험
2. 호위하다, 호위
3. 예상, 기대
4. 큰 일, 대단한 것
5. 변함없이
6. 수치심, 부끄러움
7. 창피함, 굴욕
8. 엘리트, 일류의, 우수한
9. 순서, 랭킹
10. 결과, 생산량
11. 안정된, 안정적인
12. 상쇄하다
13. 심각한 손상, 마비시키는
14. 소득기준상환
15. 연결, 관련성
16. 대기만성, 늦깎이
17. 정책
18. 시스템
19. 명문, 명성
20. 추리, 추론, 논리
21. 뱀의 머리 / 용의 꼬리
22. 출세가도, 빠른 출세길
23. 뒤처지다
24. 눈에 띄는, 현저한, 인상적인
25. 축적하는
26. 지식을 위한 지식
27. 증명서, 자격을 수여하다

숙어 및 표현

1. 빠지다
2. 난관을 이겨내다
3. 그때 그때 배우다
4. 재빨리 대응하다
5. 최고 중 최고
6. 생각해 볼 일, 생각해 볼만한 것
7. 곰곰이 생각할 거리
8. 모든 길은 로마 / 서울로 연결된다

빈칸 채우기

1. Elite
2. Crippling
3. Prestige
4. Stable
5. Credentials

반대의 의미 단어 찾기

1. e
2. c
3. a
4. d
5. b

대화 시작 질문

1. 당신 나라에 있는 상위 10개 대학은 무엇인가?
   그들의 전문성은 무엇인가?
2. 아시아에 있는 세 나라 중 최상위 세 개 대학교 이름은
   무엇인가?
3. 무엇이 대학교를 세계수준 혹은 명문으로 만드는가?
4. 왜 많은 한국인들에게 명문대에 들어가는 것이
   매우 중요한가?
5. 명문대와 일반 학교에 들어가는 것 사이에는
   어떤 차이가 있는가?
6. 명문대가 비용의 가치가 있는가? (그렇다면) 이유는? /
   (그렇지 않다면)이유는?
7. 글래드웰의 논리인 덜 유명한 학교에 가는 것에
   동의하는가?
8. 당신은 왜 당신의 학교와 전공을 골랐는가?
9. 당신은 당신의 학교에 무엇을 기여했는가?
10. 대학교생활로부터 당신이 최대한도로 배운 것은 무엇인가?

과제

위에 주어진 단어와 숙어를 가지고 문장을 만드시오.

수업 아이디어

세계적으로 가장 널리 쓰이는 세 가지 대학 순위표를 조사하라.
100개 목록을 비교하라. 그 결과 흥미로운 점은 무엇인가?
놀랍다고 생각되는 것이 있는가?

Unit 14

EQ or IQ?

Put on your thinking cap for a moment and consider what is more important for success, emotional intelligence quotient (EQ), or intelligence quotient (IQ)? Someone who is intelligent is known to be logical while having a high capacity to learn new things. Emotional intelligence, on the other hand, is to know how others feel as well as highly self-monitoring one's emotions to guide behavior.

Intelligence is useful for solving new problems or creating new ideas but if you do not have the ability to get along with others, it hinders your chances for success. Being highly intelligent but lacking empathy can lead to a reputation as being arrogant. If colleagues label you as arrogant, they can resort to nasty retaliations such as spreading untrue gossip and rumors or otherwise try to bring you down. However, if you are considerate of others and relate to how they feel, they may help you whenever possible, and come to you for advice and help. The key point in EQ is to be highly self-aware and aware of others. If you are emotionally intelligent, people are more likely to engage you for a mutually beneficial give and take relationship.

Following are some examples of being emotionally intelligent. When someone interrupts you in a meeting, ignores you in front of peers, or disrespects you in some way, you take the high road and win control over the situation. Instead of stewing about it or plotting revenge, you consider the fact that their day might have been upside down because of a fight at home with their spouse or because their boss insulted them at work. The point is giving folks the benefit of doubt and not to take things personal. Of course, this is easier said than done but those with high EQ understand that everybody has quirks and that being understanding and nice is not only important for success but also for one's own happiness.

EQ's importance is even more pronounced in some cultures. Asian countries are high-context cultures, meaning many things are left unsaid, and open to interpretation. In this environment, reading other's emotions and their poker faces is a premium skill in navigating your way to success. Those from western countries are probably more familiar with the low-context culture. In this environment, it is usually more advantageous to assert oneself and shoot straight from the hip to make sure everyone understands the situation, instead of trying to read other's feelings.

Naturally, some of us are more emotionally aware than others but EQ is a learnable skill. If you are curious to know your predisposition toward emotions or logic, take the Myers–Briggs Personality test, which is given by 80 out of the top Fortune 100 companies and taken by over 2.5 million people a year. The personality types are based on extroversion or introversion; sensing or intuition; thinking or feeling; and judging or perceiving. Regardless of your leaning, it is safe to say that all can benefit by working on EQ in addition to IQ.

- Key Vocabulary
- Idioms and Expressions

해석

EQ 또는 IQ?

성공에 있어 무엇이 더 중요한지, 감성지능인지 혹은 지능 지수인지 잠시 심사숙고 해보아라. 지능이 높은 사람은 논리적이며 새로운 것을 배우는 능력이 높다고 알려져 있다. 반면 감정 지능은 행동을 인도하기 위해 고도의 자기 점검을 하는 것뿐만 아니라 남들의 감정 또한 아는 것이다.
지능은 새로운 문제를 해결하는데 또는 새로운 아이디어를 생각하는데 유용하다. 그러나 만약 당신이 사람들과 어울리는 능력이 없다면 그것은 당신이 성공할 수 있는 기회를 방해한다. 지능은 높지만 감정이입의 부족은 오만하다는 평가를 이끌어 낼 수도 있다. 만약 동료들이 당신에게 오만하다는 딱지를 붙인다면 그들은 거짓 소문을 퍼뜨리고 그 외에 너를 끌어내리려고 하는 못된 보복을 행사할 것이다. 그러나 만약 당신이 다른 사람들을 배려하고 그들이 어떻게 느끼는지 이해한다면, 그들은 언제든지 가능할 때 당신을 도와줄 것이고 당신에게 조언과 도움을 구하러 올 것이다. 요점은 EQ는 고도로 자기를 인식하고 남을 인식한다. 만약 당신이 정서적이라면, 사람들은 당신을 서로 이득이 되는 주고받는 관계에 끌어들일 것이다.
아래에 정서적으로 행동하는 몇 가지 예가 있다. 누군가가 회의 중에 방해하고, 무리 앞에서 당신을 무시하고, 혹은 당신에게 어떤 점에 있어서 무례할 때 당신은 도덕적으로 올바른 태도를 취하고 상황의 주도권을 잡아라. 속을 태우거나 복수를 계획하는 것 대신에, 집에서 배우자와 싸우거나 직장에서 상사에게 받는 모욕 때문에 그들의 날이 엉망진창이었을 수도 있다고 생각하라. 요점은 사람들을 좋게 봐주고 기분 나쁘게 받아들이지 않는 것이다. 물론 이것은 행동보다야 말이 쉽다. 그러나 EQ가 높은 사람들은 누구나 별난 점을 가지고 있다는 것을 이해한다. 그리고 이해하고 친절하게 대하는 것은 성공을 위하여 중요할 뿐만 아니라 개인의 행복을 위해서도 중요하다.
EQ의 중요성은 몇몇 문화에서 더 확연하다. 아시아 문화들은 말하지 않은 채로 많은 것을 남겨놓고 해석하기 나름인 것을 의미하는 고(高) 맥락의 문화이다. 이 환경에서 남들의 감정과 무표정을 읽는 것은 성공으로 가는 당신의 길을 찾는 것에 있어서 고급 기술이다. 서양 사람들은 저(低) 맥락의 문화에 더 익숙하다. 이 환경에서 남의 감정을 읽는 대신 모든 사람들이 상황을 이해할 수 있게 자신을 주장하고 솔직히 얘기하는 것이 보통 더 이롭다.
물론, 우리들 중 누군가는 다른 사람들보다 감정적으로 더 잘 알아챈다. 하지만 EQ는 배울 수 있는 기술이다. 만약에 당신이 너의 성향이 정서적인지 논리적인지 궁금하다면 포춘 100개 기업 중 80개 이상의 기업이 실시하며 1년에 2백 50만명이 사용하는 MB테스트를 해보아라. 성격 타입은 외향성 혹은 내향성; 감지 혹은 직관; 생각 혹은 느낌; 그리고 판단 혹은 자각에 근거한다. 너의 성향에 상관없이, IQ에 추가하여 EQ를 개발하는 것이 일하는데 이익이 된다고 말할 수 있다.

Unit 14. EQ or IQ?

Key Vocabulary and Phrases

1. High capacity
2. Highly self-monitoring
3. Guide
4. Empathy
5. Reputation
6. Arrogant
7. Label
8. Colleague
9. Resort
10. Retaliation
11. Gossip
12. Rumor
13. Considerate
14. Give and take
15. Interrupt
16. Stew
17. Plotting
18. Not take things personal
19. Insult
20. Pronounced
21. High-context culture
22. Premium
23. Navigating
24. Low-context culture
25. Predisposition
26. Myers–Briggs test
27. Leaning
28. Self-aware
29. Mutually beneficial

Idioms and Expressions

1. Benefit of the doubt
2. Put on your thinking cap
3. Bringing you down
4. Taking the high road
5. Poker Face
6. Shoot straight from the hip
7. Safe to say
8. Upside down day

Unit 14. EQ or IQ?

Fill in the blanks with the appropriate word

1. Spreading untrue ___________ is illegal in many countries.

2. My wife ____________ my meeting by calling me to bring home milk and bread.

3. _____________ can seriously harm the reputation of a good man.

4. Even when you are angry, you should not ______________ to violence.

5. I help you and you help me is sort of like a _______________ relationship.

Match the word with the one that shows its opposite meaning

1. Insult	**a)** Disinclined
2. Predisposed	**b)** Pardon
3. Self-aware	**c)** Flattery
4. Retaliate	**d)** Proof
5. Rumors	**e)** Uninformed

Explore Further

On YouTube listen to the TED talk by Daniel Goleman

Why Aren't We All Good Samaritans?

Conversation Questions

1. What is more important to success, IQ or EQ?
2. Define intelligence. Define emotional intelligence.
3. How would your professors describe you in terms of EQ and IQ?
4. How would your friends describe you in terms of EQ and IQ?
5. When did you make a big mistake? How did you react?
6. Describe a time when you had to deliver difficult news.
7. How well do you understand other's feelings?
   What about people from different cultures?
8. How do you build relationships with new people?
9. Are IQ and EQ based on genetics or environment?
10. Does speaking English make you more intelligent than a friend who does not speak English?
11. Who is the most intelligent person you know?

Assignment

Write a sentence using each of the key vocabulary word and idiom given above.

Unit 14. EQ or IQ?

Vocabulary

1.
2.
3.
4.
5.
6.
7.
8.
9.
10.
11.
12.
13.
14.
15.
16.
17.
18.
19.
20.
21.

22.

23.

24.

25.

26.

27.

28.

29.

Idioms

1.

2.

3.

4.

5.

6.

7.

8.

Class Idea

Take the Myers–Briggs test or equivalent on-line. Does the test accurately describe your personality? Which celebrity has a similar personality?

Unit 14. EQ or IQ?

Definition of Key Words

- **Empathy** n. — the feeling that you understand and share another person's experiences and emotions; the ability to share someone else's feelings; *He felt great empathy with the poor.*
  Origin: Greek, first known use in 1850

- **Reputation** n. — the common opinion that people have about someone or something; the way in which people think of someone or something;
  He has earned a reputation for being a good fighter.
  Synonyms: character, fame, mark, name
  Origin: Middle English, from Anglo-French, first known use in the 14th century

- **Arrogant** adj. — having or showing the insulting attitude of people who believe that they are better, smarter, or more important than other people; having or showing arrogance;
  She's first in her class, but she's not arrogant about it.
  Synonyms: assumptive, haughty, lofty, uppity, pompous
  Origin: Middle English, from Latin, first known use in the 14th century

- **Resort** n. — a place where people go for vacations; something that you choose for help;
  Our first resort was to go to the police.

- **Resort** v. — to go especially frequently or habitually; to have recourse;
  He is known for resorting to violence to solve his problems.
  Origin: first known use in the 15th century

- **Retaliate** v. — to do something bad to someone who has hurt you or treated you badly; to get revenge against someone;
  He retaliated against his neighbor's loud noise by calling the police.
  Origin: Late Latin, first known use in 1611

- **Gossip** n. — information about the behavior and personal lives of other people; information about the lives of famous people; a person who often talks about the private details of other people's lives;
  He had been spreading gossip about his coworkers.

- **Gossip** v. — to talk about the personal lives of other people; *They often gossip about their classmates.*
  Origin: Middle English, first known use before the 12th century

- **Rumor** n. information or a story that is passed from person to person but has not been proven to be true; *There are rumors that they are making a new film.*
  Synonyms: buzz, dish, gossip, hearsay, report
  Origin: Middle English, from Anglo-French, first known use in the 14th century

- **Interrupt** v. to ask questions or say things while another person is speaking; to cause something to stop happening for a time; to cause something to not be even or continuous; *It's not polite to interrupt.*
  Synonyms: break in, chime in, chip in, intrude
  Origin: Middle English, from Latin, first known use in the 15th century

- **Plot** n. an area of land that is considered a unit; a series of events from a story in a novel, movie, etc.; *They just bought a 12-acre plot of land.*

- **Plot** v. to plan secretly to do something usually illegal or harmful; to plan something; to mark something on a map, graph, chart, etc.; *They plotted to steal the painting.*
  Synonyms: collude, compass, connive, conspire, scheme
  Origin: Middle English, from Old English, first known use in the 12th century

- **Insult** v. to do or say something that is offensive; to do or say something that shows a lack of respect for someone; *We were greatly insulted by his rudeness.*
  Synonyms: affront, disrespect, offend, outrage, wound
  Origin: Middle French or Latin, first known use in 1540

- **Premium** n. the price of insurance; a price that is higher than the regular price; a high or extra value; *Health insurance premiums went up again this year.*
  Synonyms: accolade, honor, award, prize
  Origin: Latin, first known use in 1601

pp. 153~157 한국어 해설

EQ 또는 IQ?

주요단어 및 구절

1. 고성능, 높은 능력
2. 고도의 자기점검
3. 인도하다
4. 감정이입, 공감
5. 평판
6. 오만한
7. 딱지를 붙이다, 꼬리표를 붙이다
8. 동료
9. 행사하다, 호소하다
10. 보복
11. 소문, 험담
12. 소문
13. 배려하는, 사려깊은
14. 타협, 교환, 주고 받다
15. 방해하다, 중단시키다
16. 화를 내다, 속을 태우다
17. 음모, 계획
18. 기분 나쁘게 받아들이지 않다
19. 모욕하다
20. 확연한, 단호한
21. 고 맥락 문화
22. 고급의
23. 길을 찾는
24. 저 맥락 문화
25. 성향, 경향
26. 마이어브릭스 테스트
27. 성향
28. 자기인식, 자각
29. 상호이익의

숙어 및 표현

1. 선의의 해석, 좋게 봐주다
2. 심사숙고하다
3. 떨어뜨리는[기], 콧대를 꺾[기]
4. 도덕적으로 올바른 태도를 취하는[기], (싸움) 차분한 태도를 취하는[기]
5. 무표정한 얼굴
6. 솔직하게 말하다, 직설적으로 말하다
7. ~라고 해도 괜찮다
8. 엉망진창인 날

빈칸 채우기

1. Rumors
2. Interrupted
3. Gossip
4. Resort
5. Give and take

반대의 의미 단어 찾기

1. c
2. a
3. e
4. b
5. d

대화 질문

1. IQ, EQ 중 무엇이 성공하는데 더 중요한가?
2. 지능을 정의하라. 정서지능을 정의하라.
3. 당신의 교수님이 EQ와 IQ면에서 당신을 어떻게 묘사하겠는가?
4. 당신의 친구들이 EQ와 IQ면에서 당신을 어떻게 묘사하겠는가?
5. 당신은 언제 큰 실수를 했는가? 어떻게 반응했는가?
6. 당신이 어려운 뉴스를 전달해야 했었을 때를 설명하라.
7. 당신은 다른 사람의 감정을 얼마나 잘 이해하는가? 다른 문화에서 온 사람들을 잘 이해 하는가?
8. 새로운 사람과 어떻게 관계를 형성하는가?
9. IQ와 EQ는 유전과 환경 중 무엇에 근거하는가?
10. 영어로 말하는 것이 영어로 말하지 못하는 친구들보다 당신을 더 똑똑하게 만드는가?
11. 당신이 아는 사람 중 가장 똑똑한 사람은 누구인가?

과제

위에 주어진 단어와 숙어를 가지고 문장을 만드시오.

수업 아이디어

마이어브릭스 시험이나 비슷한 시험을 온라인으로 보아라. 시험이 정확히 당신의 성격을 말해 주는가? 비슷한 성격을 가진 유명인사는 누구인가?

The Self-Made

According to a Bloomberg report, 60% of the world's billionaires were once poor. Everyone enjoys a rags to riches tale because we all hope to believe you can make it if you work hard enough. Millionaire hip-hop rapper Drake once said that the first million is the hardest. Businessman T. Boone Pickens on Twitter replied that "the first billion is a helluva lot harder." But is the American dream or the Korean dream or the Chinese dream really alive for the rest of us?

Some claim that the U.S. is an oligarchy in which the wealth and the power of the country belong to a small number of people. These people or the so-called upper crust are distinguished by wealth, family ties, education, and the good ol' boy network. Without a doubt, the U.S. is supposed to be a democracy where power is to be with the people but naysayers say only the rich look out for their interests, whereas the middle class withers away.

Inequality of wealth is indeed a serious matter of contention. Yet, there are always two sides to a coin. To play devil's advocate, consider a question from Fox conservative TV host Bill O'Reilly and liberal President Barack Hussein Obama. He asked Mr. President, "How can you try and radically change a country that has given you all the opportunity you received?" In fact, President Obama came from a single-parent home, middle-class family, and with a strange sounding name to become the first black president of the U.S.

Does that mean people still have the opportunity to be self-made? Are those billionaires and millionaires self-made? Is it true that they are just smarter than the rest or that they just worked harder than the rest? If the system really is a meritocracy where people have a fair shake at getting ahead, then perhaps people really are self-made. Or perhaps people are aided by the sheer luck of being at the right place, at the right time, and in the right country with the right skills. As Malcom Gladwell once wrote, perhaps none of the outliers who ever became rich ever made it all on his/her own.

- Key Vocabulary
- Idioms and Expressions

해석

자수성가

블룸버그 보고서에 따르면 세계 억만장자 중 60%는 가난했었다. 열심히 일을 하면 해낼 수 있다고 모두가 믿길 원하기 때문에 무일푼에서 부자가 된 이야기를 좋아한다. 백만장자 힙합가수 드레이크는 "처음 백만이 가장 힘들었다."라고 말했다. 사업가 티 분 피켄스는 "처음 십억이 훨씬 더 지독하게 힘들다."라고 트위터에 답변했다. 그러나 아메리칸 드림 혹은 코리아 드림 혹은 차이니즈 드림은 정말 나머지 사람인 우리를 위해 존재할까?
어떤 사람들은 미국이 국가의 부와 권력이 몇몇 소수의 사람들에게 속해있는 과두정부라고 주장한다. 이 사람들 또는 소위 상류층이라 불리는 사람들은 부, 가족관계, 교육 그리고 학연으로 구별된다. 의심할 여지없이 미국은 권력이 대중들에게 있는 민주주의여야 하지만 중산층이 약해지는 반면 부자들만이 그들의 이익을 지킨다고 반대론자들은 말한다.
부의 불평등은 심각한 논쟁거리이다. 여전히 동전은 항상 양면이 있다. 일부러 반대 의견을 말해보기 위해 FOX의 보수적 TV 호스트 빌 오라일리 그리고 진보적 대통령 버락 후세인 오바마 양측 모두의 질문을 생각해보아라. 빌 오라일리는 대통령에게 "어떻게 당신에게 모든 기회를 준 나라를 이렇게 갑작스럽게 바꿀 수 있습니까?"라고 물었다. 사실, 대통령 오바마는 중산층의 편부모하에서 자랐고, 이상하게 들리는 이름은 미국 최초의 흑인 대통령이 되었다.
이것은 사람들이 아직 자수성가 할 수 있는 기회가 있다는 의미인가? 이런 억만장자 백만장자들이 자수성가하였나? 그들이 단지 나머지 사람들 보다 똑똑하고 일을 더 열심히 했다는 것이 사실인가? 만약 시스템이 정말 사람들이 앞으로 나아갈 수 있는 공평한 기회가 있는 실력주의라면, 어쩌면 사람들은 자수성가할 수도 있다. 아니면 어쩌면 사람들은 순전히 올바른 자리에, 올바른 시간에, 올바른 기술이 있는 올바른 국가에 속해 있다는, 천운의 도움을 받는지도 모른다. 말콤 글래드웰이 썼던 것처럼, 아마도 큰 성공을 거둔 사람들 중 그 누구도 온전히 혼자만의 힘으로 부자가 된 것은 아닐 것이다.

Unit 15. The Self-Made

Key Vocabulary and Phrases

1. Bloomberg
2. Millionaire
3. Rapper
4. Billionaire
5. American Dream
6. Oligarchy
7. Upper crust
8. Without a doubt
9. Democracy
10. Naysayer
11. Wither
12. Inequality of wealth
13. Contention
14. Conservative
15. Liberal
16. Radically
17. Single-parent home
18. Middle class
19. Self-made
20. Meritocracy
21. Sheer
22. Outlier
23. Make it on their own

Idioms and Expressions

1. Rags to riches
2. Good ol' boy network
3. Two sides to a coin
4. Devil's advocate
5. Fair shake at getting ahead

Unit 15. The Self-Made

Fill in the blanks with the appropriate word

1. Bill Gates and Warren Buffett are ________________.

2. Eminem is a famous ________________.

3. A small group of people control Russia's economy and so they are ________________.

4. ________________ is the type of government where power comes from the people.

5. The tallest man in the world is almost 8 feet tall. He is a true _____________.

Match the word with the one that shows its opposite meaning

1. Meritocracy	**a)** Privileged
2. Outlier	**b)** Elite
3. Self-made	**c)** Conservative
4. Middle-class	**d)** Socialist
5. Radical	**e)** Average

Conversation Starters

1. Is there a difference between someone who is self-made and someone born with a silver spoon in their mouth if both are equally rich?

2. What drives people to achieve great success?

3. How much of a role does luck play in success?

4. How important is success to you and why?

5. What steps do you have to take to reach your goals?

6. Should the rich pay more tax than they are paying now? If so, why?

7. Do the rich have more responsibility or debt to society than others?

8. Do the poor and the middle class have a fair chance of getting ahead in society? If not, why do you think so?

9. Is having knowledge more important than receiving a windfall of wealth? Please explain.

10. What is more important, having much wealth or having many good friends?

Assignment

Write a sentence using each of the vocabulary and idiom given above.

Vocabulary

1. ______

2. ______

3. ______

4. ______

5. ______

6. ______

7. ______

8. ______

Unit 15. The Self-Made

9.

10.

11.

12.

13.

14.

15.

16.

17.

18.

19.

20.

21.

22.

23.

Idioms

1.

2.

3.

4.

5.

Definition of Key Words

- **Oligarchy** n. a county, business, etc., that is controlled by a small group of people; the people that control a country, business, etc.; *Their nation is an oligarchy.*
  Origin: first known use in 1542

- **Upper crust** n. the highest social class or group; the highest circle of the upper class; *The prices are high since the store targets the upper-crust.*
  Synonyms: aristocracy, best, illuminati, royalty
  Origin: first known use in 1836

- **Self-made** n. made rich and successful by your own efforts; *Steve Jobs was a self-made man.*
  Origin: first known use in 1615

- **Naysayer** n. a person who says something will not work or is not possible; a person who denies, refuses, or opposes something; *There are always naysayers who say it can't be done.*
  Synonyms: pessimist, doubter, hater
  Origin: first known use in 1721

- **Wither** v. of a plant: to become dry and weak; to lose vitality, force, or freshness; *The plants withered and died.*
  Synonyms: dry, wilt
  Origin: Middle English, first known use in the 14th century

- **Contention** n. something that is argued or stated; anger and disagreement; a situation in which you have chance to win something that you are trying to win; *That has been a source of contention for years.*
  Synonyms: argument, assertion, thesis
  Origin: Middle English, from Anglo-French, first known use in the 14th century

- **Liberal** adj. believing that government should be active in supporting social and political change; marked by generosity; *She is a liberal Democrat who married a conservative Republican.*
  Synonyms: broad-minded, nonconventional, open-minded, progressive, radical
  Origin: Middle English, from Anglo-French, first known use in the 14th century

Unit 15. The Self-Made

- **Radical** adj. very new and different from what is traditional or ordinary; very basic and important;
  having extreme political or social views that are not shared by most people;
  The computer has introduced radical innovations.

- **Radical** n. a person who favors extreme changes in government;
  a person who has radical political opinions;
  He was a radical when he was young.
  Synonyms: extreme, revolutionary, ultra, extremist
  Origin: first known use in 1641

- **Meritocracy** n. a system in which the talented are chosen and moved ahead on the basis of their achievement;
  leadership selected on the basis of intellectual criteria;
  Does a meritocracy lead to inequality in a society?
  Origin: first known use in 1958

- **Sheer** v. to deviate from a course; *The car sheered to avoid hitting the dog.*

- **Sheer** adj. use to emphasize the large amount, size, or degree of something; complete and total;
  The neighbors could see right through our sheer curtains.
  Origin: Middle English, from Old Norse, first known use in 1568

- **Outliers** n. a person whose residence and place of business are at a distance;
  a statistical observation that is markedly different in value from the others of the sample;
  Bill Gates and Warren Buffet are true outliers because of their wealth.
  Origin: first known use in 1676

pp. 163~165 한국어 해설

자수성가

주요단어 및 구절

1. 블룸버그 회사
2. 백만장자
3. 래퍼, 랩 가수
4. 억만장자
5. 아메리칸 드림
   (미국에 가면 무슨 일을 하든 행복하게 잘살 수 있으리라는 생각)
6. 과두정부
7. 상류층
8. 틀림없이, 의심할 여지 없이
9. 민주주의
10. 반대론자, 비관론자
11. 시들다, 약해지다
12. 부의 불평등
13. 논쟁, 언쟁
14. 보수적인
15. 진보적인, 자유민주적인
16. 급진적으로
17. 편부모 가정
18. 중산층 (middle-class 중산층의)
19. 자수성가한
20. 실력주의
21. 순전한, 완전히
22. 큰 성공을 거둔사람, 표본 중 다른 대상들과 확연히 구분되는 것
23. 스스로 헤쳐나가다

숙어 및 표현

1. 무일푼에서 부자로
2. 학연
3. 동전의 양면
4. 일부러 반대 입장을 말하다
5. 앞으로 나갈 수 있는 공정한 기회

빈칸 채우기

1. Billionaires
2. Rapper
3. Oligarchs
4. Democracy
5. Outlier

반대의 의미 단어 찾기

1. d
2. e
3. a
4. b
5. c

대화 질문

1. 자수성가한 사람과 부잣집에서 태어난 사람이 똑같이 부자라면 차이가 있는가?
2. 무엇이 사람들이 대성공을 이루게 하는가?
3. 성공에 있어서 운은 얼마나 많은 작용을 하는가?
4. 당신에게 성공은 얼마나 그리고 왜 중요한가?
5. 당신의 목표를 이루기 위해 어떤 단계를 밟아야 하는가?
6. 부자는 세금을 지금 내는 것 보다 많이 내야 하는가? 만약 그렇다면 이유는?
7. 부자들이 다른 사람들보다 사회에 대한 책임이나 빚이 더 많은가?
8. 빈곤층과 중산층이 사회에서 앞으로 나아갈 공정한 기회가 있는가? 그렇지 않다면, 왜 그렇게 생각하는가?
9. 지식을 얻는 것이 뜻밖의 횡재로 부자가 되는 것보다 더 중요한가? 설명하라.
10. 많은 부를 갖는 것 또는 많은 좋은 친구들을 갖는 것 중에 무엇이 더 중요한가?

과제

위에 주어진 단어와 숙어를 가지고 문장을 만드시오.

Unit 16

Are the Rich Different?

It is difficult to come to grips with how the rich are different. Ostensibly, they are not cut from the same cloth. An interview with gambling tycoon Sheldon Adelson sheds light on one divergence. A reporter asked how he felt about his immense fortune. He answered it feels pretty special to be richer than 99.999999 or whatever percentage of humans present on the planet. The reporter then asked what he wants to do with all of his wealth. He said he only cared for the people he can know or see; that he did not care to share wealth with far apart descendants of the future.

Bill Gates, a college dropout and a computer geek, has also stated plans to use his vast fortune to solve problems instead of leaving his wealth to his children. He considers such a windfall to children as more of a burden than a gift. Warren Buffet has similar plans and is famous for his penny-pinching and frugality. He still lives in the home he purchased for $31,500 in 1957. While Bill Gates and Warren Buffet are stellar examples of thrifty living and philanthropy, other tycoons have a different take. One of the richest men in the world, Carlos Slim said he does not believe in charities. Despite forking over a lot of money to different charities, he believes he can do more to fight poverty by building businesses than by "being a Santa Claus."

Giving away wealth by the super rich in the U.S. is nothing new. Andrew Carnegie in his book "The Gospel of Wealth" argued that there is a much greater benefit to society by giving away wealth than by handing it down to heirs or by living an extravagant life. Carnegie himself established libraries across the U.S. and some of his contemporaries such as John Rockefeller and Leland Stanford helped start the University of Chicago and Stanford University along with Johns Hopkins who started Johns Hopkins University. There are many examples of the supremely wealthy doing well for society; but is this their mandatory social responsibility?

Besides their power and giving, the rich have different habits. Most own a business that acts as a cash cow. Moreover, if something costs an arm and a leg just because of the brand image, they will probably move on. If they are involved in a losing business venture, they are more likely to cut their losses and walk away, not falling into the sunken costs fallacy where one gets emotionally entangled investing more into a failing project depending on how much time and effort they have already invested.

Maybe the rich are different. Their spending habits, thinking, and lifestyles are night and day from the average Joe. At the end of the day though, if you remember that a penny saved is a penny earned, and to never put all of your investment eggs into one basket, you may have the chance to live a life without financial debt or stress. Whether rich or not, the key is to being happy and satisfied with life. Get there by focusing on the things that excite you and give you joy.

• Key Vocabulary

• Idioms and Expressions

해석

부자는 다른가?

부자들이 어떻게 다른지 이해하기는 어렵다. 표면상으로, 그들은 본바탕이 같지 않다. 도박계의 거부 셸던 아델슨은 인터뷰에서 한가지 차이점을 밝혔다. 리포터가 그의 엄청난 재산에 대해 어떻게 생각하느냐고 물었다. 그는 다른 99%보다 혹은 지구 상에 존재하는 사람들 중 몇 퍼센트가 됐든지 그들보다 더 부자인 것은 꽤나 특별하다고 말했다. 다음으로 리포터는 그 많은 돈을 가지고 무얼 하기를 원하는지 물었다. 그는 오직 자신이 아는 사람들에게만 신경 쓸 것이라고 했다. 그는 미래의 먼 자손들과 부를 나눌 생각은 없다고 밝혔다.

대학 중퇴자 그리고 컴퓨터 괴짜 빌게이츠는, 역시 그의 거대한 재산을 그의 아이들에게 남기는 대신 많은 문제들을 해결하는데 사용하겠다는 계획을 언급했다. 그가 이런 큰 횡재는 아이들에게 선물이기보다는 큰 짐이라고 생각한다. 구두쇠 그리고 절약으로 유명한 워렌 버핏도 비슷한 계획들을 가지고 있다. 그는 그가 1957년 31,500달러에 구매한 집에 여전히 살고 있다. 빌게이츠와 워렌 버핏이 절약하는 생활과 자선활동의 뛰어난 예인 반면 다른 거부들은 다르다. 세계에서 가장 부자 중 한 명인 카를로스 슬림은 그는 자선활동을 믿지 않는다고 밝혔다. 많은 돈을 다른 자선단체들에게 기부하는 데에도 불구하고, 그는 "산타클로스가 되는 것"보다 사업체를 세우는 것이 가난과 더 싸울 수 있다고 믿는다.

미국의 최고 부자들이 돈을 사회에 기부하는 것은 새로운 게 아니다. 앤드류 카네기는 그의 책 〈부의 복음〉에서 부를 상속인에게 물려주거나 사치스러운 삶을 사는 것보다 사회에 부를 환원하는 것이 사회에 훨씬 더 좋은 이익이 있다고 주장했다. 카네기는 그 스스로 미국 전역에 도서관을 설립하였고 록펠러나 스탠포드 같은 그의 동시대 사람들 몇몇도 존 홉킨스가 존 홉킨스 대학을 시작한 것과 마찬가지로 시카고 대학 그리고 스탠포드 대학을 시작했다. 극도의 부자들이 사회를 위하여 실천한 많은 예가 있다. 그러나 이것이 그들의 의무적 사회 책임인가?

그들의 권력과 기부 외에도, 부자들은 다른 습관들을 가지고 있다. 대부분의 부자들은 고수익 사업을 가지고 있다. 게다가 만약 어떤 것이 단지 브랜드 이미지로 인해 엄청난 비용이 든다면 그들은 아마 그냥 지나갈 것이다. 만약 그들이 승산이 없는 투기적 사업에 참여했다면, 그들이 얼마나 많은 시간과 노력을 이미 투자했는지에 따라 감정적이 되어 실패한 계획에 더 투자하는 매몰비용 오류에 빠지지 않고 그들은 손실을 줄이고 떠나 버리는 경향이 많다.

부자들은 어쩌면 다르다. 그들의 소비 습관, 생각 그리고 생활방식은 평균적인 사람과 완전히 다르다. 결국 당신이 만약 티끌 모아 태산 그리고 절대 한 곳에 모두 투자하지 않는다는 것을 기억한다면 당신은 아마 재정적인 빚이나 스트레스가 없는 삶을 살 수 있을 것이다. 부자이든 아니든 요점은 삶에 만족하고 행복해지는 것이다. 당신을 신나게 하는 것 당신에게 즐거움을 주는 것에 집중하여 행복하고 만족스러운 삶을 이루어라.

Unit 16. Are the Rich Different?

Key Vocabulary and Phrases

1. Tycoon
2. Divergence
3. Immense
4. Fortune
5. Dropout
6. Geek
7. Frugality
8. Stellar
9. Philanthropy
10. Charity
11. Poverty
12. Being a Santa Claus
13. Heir
14. Extravagant
15. Contemporary
16. Supremely
17. Mandatory
18. Sunken Costs Fallacy
19. Entangled
20. Ostensible

Idioms and Expressions

1. Come to grips (with)
2. Shed light on
3. Penny-pinching
4. A different take
5. Forking over
6. Cash cow
7. Costing an arm and a leg
8. Average Joe
9. Eggs in one basket
10. Night and day
11. Cut from the same cloth

Unit 16. Are the Rich Different?

Fill in the blanks with the appropriate word

1. He rose up from ___________ and became rich.

2. Famous athletes often live ___________ lives and end up broke.

3. To get an A in this class, it is ___________ that you show up for every class.

4. A liar often gets _______________ in their web of lies.

5. American ___________ are known for some of the greatest philanthropy around the world, such as the Bill and Melinda Gates Foundation.

Match the word with the one that shows its opposite meaning

1. Poverty	**a)** Voluntary
2. Mandatory	**b)** Debt
3. Frugality	**c)** Lavishness
4. Fortune	**d)** Luxury
5. Ostensible	**e)** Vague

Conversation Questions

1. If you get a chance to lunch with Warren Buffett what would you ask him?
2. Are you jealous of rich people?
3. Are the rich more selfish than ordinary people?
4. What would you do with incredible wealth? Tell us your to-do list.
5. Would you give away your wealth like Bill Gates or pass it on to your family?
6. Who is the richest person you know? Does he/she have any particular quirks?
7. Should the rich donate money to charities or start more businesses? Which is better for society and why?
8. What are the best and worst things about being wealthy?
9. What are the genuine reasons for people wanting to be wealthy?
10. Do you know anyone who lost a lot of wealth? How did he/she change?
11. What are you enthusiastic about?

Assignment

Write a sentence using each of the key vocabulary word and idiom given above.

Explore Further

On YouTube listen to the TED talk by Chrystia Freeland

The Rise of the New Global Super-Rich

Unit 16. Are the Rich Different?

Vocabulary

1.
2.
3.
4.
5.
6.
7.
8.
9.
10.
11.
12.
13.
14.
15.
16.
17.
18.
19.
20.

Idioms

1.
2.
3.
4.
5.
6.
7.
8.
9.
10.
11.

Definition of Key Words

- **Tycoon** n. a very wealthy and powerful business person;
  Carlos Slim is a telecommunications tycoon.
  Origin: Japanese taikun, first known use in 1857

- **Divergence** n. a drawing apart; a deviation from a course or standard;
  the condition of being mathematically divergent;
  There is a growing divergence of opinion in the U.S. on gay marriages.
  Synonyms: bifurcation, separation, divarication
  Origin: first known use in 1656

Unit 16. Are the Rich Different?

- Geek n. a person who is socially awkward and unpopular;
  a usually intelligent person who does not fit in with other people;
  a person who is very interested in and knows a lot about a particular field or activity;
  He was a real geek in high school.
  Synonyms: dork, nerd, bookworm, dink
  Origin: English from German, first known use in 1914

- Inheritance n. money, property, etc., that is received from someone when that person dies;
  something from the past that is still important or valuable;
  the act of inheriting something;
  He left sizable inheritances to his children.
  Synonyms: bequest, heritage, legacy, patrimony
  Origin: first known use in the 14th century

- Frugal adj. careful about spending money or using things when you do not need to;
  using money or supplies in a very careful way; simple and plain;
  He ate a frugal meal of bread and cheese.
  Synonyms: economical, thrifty, sparing
  Origin: Middle French or Latin, first known use in 1590

- Stellar adj. of or relating to the stars; very good; *The movie has a stellar cast.*
  Synonyms: star, starry
  Origin: Latin, first known use in 1656

- Philanthropy n. the practice of giving money and time to help make life better for other people;
  The family's philanthropy made it possible to build the public library.
  Synonyms: alms, charity, donation
  Origin: Latin, from Greek, first known use in 1623

- Heir n. a person who has the legal right to receive the property of someone who dies;
  a person who has the right to become a king or queen or to claim a title when the person holding it dies; *His heirs could inherit millions of dollars.*
  Synonyms: heir at law, inheritor
  Origin: Middle English, from Anglo-French, first known use in the 13th century

- **Extravagant** adj. more than is usual, necessary, or proper; very fancy; very expensive and not necessary;
  Her extravagant spending has to stop.
  Synonyms: prodigal, spendthrift, thriftless, wasteful
  Origin: Middle English, from Middle French, first known use in the 15th century

- **Contemporary** adj. happening or beginning now or in recent times; existing or happening in the same time period;
  GQ is a magazine devoted to contemporary fashions.

- **Contemporary** n. a person who lives at the same time or is about the same age as another person;
  He was a contemporary of George Washington.
  Synonyms: coexisting, coincidental, synchronic, concurrent
  Origin: Latin, first known use in 1631

- **Mandatory** adj. required by a law or rule; *The tests are mandatory for all students wishing to graduate.*
  Synonyms: compulsory, forced, imperative, incumbent, necessary
  Origin: first known use in the 15th century

- **Entangled** v. to cause something to get caught in or twisted with something else;
  to get someone involved in a confusing or difficult situation;
  The young runaway gradually became entangled in a life of crime.
  Synonyms: interlace, knot, tangle, snarl
  Origin: Middle English, from Anglo-French, first known use in the 15th century

- **Ostensible** adj. seeming or said to be true or real but very possibly not true or real;
  The ostensible reason for the meeting turned out to be a trick to get him to the surprise party.
  Synonyms: assumed, evident, apparent, ostensive, presumed
  Origin: French, from Latin, first known use in 1771

pp. 173~175 한국어 해설

부자는 다른가?

주요단어 및 구절

1. 거물, 재벌
2. 차이
3. 엄청난
4. 재산, 부 / 행운
5. 중퇴자, 중퇴
6. 괴짜
7. 절약, 검소
8. 뛰어난, 별의
9. 자선활동, 자선사업
10. 자선단체, 자선
11. 가난, 빈곤
12. 산타클로스가 되는 것
13. 상속인
14. 낭비하는, 사치스러운
15. 동시대인(人), 동시대의
16. 극도로, 지극히
17. 의무적인
18. 매몰 비용 오류
19. 얽힌
20. 표면적으로는

숙어 및 표현

1. 이해하다
2. 비추다, 해명하다, 밝히다
3. 구두쇠의, 인색한 (penny-pincher 구두쇠)
4. 다른, 다름
5. 넘겨주는[기], 지불하는[기]
6. 고수익 상품
7. 엄청나게 비싼
8. 평균적인 사람
9. 한가지 일에 모든 것을 걸다 (올 인하다)
10. 밤낮으로, 전혀
11. 매우 비슷한

빈칸 채우기

1. Poverty
2. Extravagant
3. Mandatory
4. Entangled
5. Tycoons

반대의 의미 단어 찾기

1. d
2. a
3. c
4. b
5. e

대화 질문

1. 만약 당신이 워렌 버핏과 점심을 먹을 수 있다면 무엇을 물어보겠는가?
2. 당신은 부자들을 질투하나?
3. 보통 사람들보다 부자들이 조금 더 이기적인가?
4. 엄청난 부가 있다면 무엇을 할 것 인가?
   당신의 해야 할 일 목록을 말해보아라.
5. 당신은 엄청난 부를 빌게이츠 같이 기부할 것인가 아니면 가족에게 상속할 것인가?
6. 당신이 아는 가장 부자는 누구인가?
   그들은 특별히 별난 점이 있는가?
7. 부자들은 자선사업체에 돈을 기부해야 하는가 아니면 사업체를 더 늘려야 하는가? 무엇이 더 사회에게 도움이 되는가? 이유는?
8. 잘 사는 것의 가장 좋은 점과 가장 나쁜 점은 무엇인가?
9. 사람들이 부를 원하는 진짜 이유는 무엇인가?
10. 많은 부를 잃어버린 사람을 알고 있는가? 그들은 어떻게 변했는가?
11. 당신은 무엇에 열광적인가?

과제

위에 주어진 단어와 숙어를 가지고 문장을 만드시오.

Unit 17

Are You an Entrepreneur?

It is common knowledge that being a successful entrepreneur calls for hard work and risk taking. Entrepreneurs spot trends in an economy and pick their shots at introducing new products or services to customers. In the early stages, most of the risks fall squarely on the entrepreneurs but with a dynamic business plan, they can seek capital from a venture capital firm or angel investors. Thus, they can spread the risk of failure and losing money to the people who invest in the company but there is no such thing as a free lunch or a walk in the park. Often, investors want some ownership of the company through stocks and want to call the shots on the future direction of the company. If you are willing to give up some control and ownership, and have the next great idea, you can fund your future business venture without personally putting everything on the line.

One successful case study on entrepreneurs is Mark Zuckerberg. He started Facebook with friends in Harvard's dormitory. Like Bill Gates, he is a dropout but still one of the world's richest people with a net worth of over 25 billion dollars. He being the CEO of the company takes only $1 as a salary. Many of people accuse Zuckerberg of stealing the idea of Facebook from others, but does that matter? As the cliché goes, it is not the first person who comes up with the idea, but the first person that can bank on it that gets the glory. I can imagine him saying to those left out, "It's just business."

A similar narrative surrounds Bill Gates, who was accused of copying other's ideas, but there is no denying his business acumen and his ability to execute a business strategy. Both Zuckerberg and Gates are self-proclaimed computer nerds and yet seem to possess the DNA of a great entrepreneur.

Israel is a nation full of entrepreneurs and start-ups. Despite its size, it can create more start-ups than any other nation, except the U.S. Conceivably, the country attributes play a part. In the book "Start-Up Nation: The Story of Israel's Economic Miracle," the authors wrote that conscription military service is filled with hi-tech hands on training that is useful for civilian life after service. Because Israel is constantly under attack without resources, it has no choice but to develop its own technologies and industries to survive.

In the film "Do The Right Thing" by Spike Lee, some African Americans asked, "How do these Koreans come here fresh off the boat and within a few years start their own business and prosper?" Perhaps without good English and the ability to get a good job, many first generation Korean Americans start their own businesses such as a fruit stand, convenience store, or restaurant. In Korea, laid off mid-level managers open up chicken restaurants in an overcrowded industry because they have to find a way to earn money after being fired. Are they entrepreneurs too? That is, is there a difference between a business owner and a real entrepreneur?

One difference with hi-tech entrepreneurs is they have an exit strategy in mind before they start their business, such as striking gold with an initial public offering (IPO) or to being in a merger and acquisition (M&A) before they go off to something else. Conversely, many small business owners just do it out of necessity and with the intention of making a good living. Are entrepreneurs different from small business owners with the former being in the big leagues or are they like two peas in a pod, just with varying degrees of success?

- Key Vocabulary
- Idioms and Expressions

해석

당신은 사업가인가?

성공적인 사업가가 되기 위해서 고생과 위험부담을 할 필요가 있다는 것은 상식이다. 사업가들은 경제에서 트렌드를 찾고, 고객에게 새로운 상품이나 서비스를 소개할 기회를 고른다. 초기 단계에는 대부분의 위험은 정확하게 사업가들 위로 떨어진다. 그러나 역동적인 사업계획서가 있다면 그들은 창업투자회사나 선의의 투자자로부터 자금을 받을 수 있는지 알아볼 수 있다. 따라서 그들은 회사에 투자한 사람들에게 실패 위험, 돈을 잃을 위험을 분산시킬 수 있다. 그러나 쉬운 일은 없다. 종종 투자자들은 주식을 통해 경영권을 원하고 회사의 미래 방향을 통제하길 원한다. 만약 당신이 약간의 지휘권이나 경영권을 포기할 의사가 있고 다른 좋은 아이디어가 있다면 당신은 미래 벤처사업에 개인적으로 모든 것을 걸지 않아도 자금을 조달할 수가 있다.

사업에서 배우는 성공적인 예는 마크 주크버그이다. 그는 하버드 기숙사에서 친구들과 페이스 북을 시작했다. 빌게이츠처럼 그는 중퇴했지만 여전히 250억 달러 이상의 순 자산을 가진 세계 최고 부자들 중 한 명이다. 그는 회사의 CEO로서 오직 1달러의 월급을 받는다. 많은 사람들이 페이스 북 아이디어를 남으로부터 훔쳤다고 주크버그를 고발한다. 그러나 그게 문제가 되는가? 상투적인 표현대로, 영광을 차지하는 사람은 아이디어를 낸 첫 번째 사람이 아니고, 그것을 확신한 첫 번째 사람이다. 난 그가 그런 배제된 사람들에게 말하는 것을 상상할 수 있다. "그건 단지 사업이야."

누군가의 아이디어를 베꼈다고 고소당했던, 비슷한 이야기로 둘러싸인 빌 게이츠, 그러나 그의 사업 감각과 사업전략을 경영하는 능력은 아무도 부인할 수 없다. 주크버그와 게이츠 모두 자칭 컴퓨터 괴짜임에도 불구하고 뛰어난 사업 DNA를 가지고 있는 듯하다.

이스라엘은 기업가와 창업자로 가득 찬 나라이다. 나라의 크기에도 불구하고 이스라엘은 미국을 제외한 다른 어떤 나라들보다 더 많은 신규업체를 만들어낸다. 생각할 수 있는 바로는 나라의 특성 덕분이다. 〈창업국가 : 이스라엘 경제의 기적〉이라는 책에서 징병제 군 복무는 복무가 끝난 다음에 민간인의 생활에 도움이 되는 실용적인 첨단 기술 훈련으로 가득 차 있다. 그리고 이스라엘은 지속적으로 자원이 없이 공격을 받고 있기 때문에 살아남기 위해 자신만의 기술과 산업을 발전시키는 것 말고는 선택의 여지가 없다.

스파이크 리의 영화 〈똑바로 살아라〉에서, 어떤 흑인은 "어떻게 한국인들은 이민 온 지 얼마 되지 않아 몇 년 만에 사업을 하고 번창할 수 있는지?" 물어본다. 아마 좋은 직장을 구할 영어실력과 능력이 없어서 많은 미국 교포 1세대는 과일가게, 편의점 혹은 식당 같은 자영업을 시작했을 것이다. 한국에서는 실직 당한 중간 매니저들이 해고당한 후 돈을 벌 수 있는 방법을 찾아야 하기에 이미 포화상태인 산업인 치킨 집을 개점한다. 그들 역시 기업가인가? 다시 말하면, 진짜 기업가와 자영업자 사이에 차이점이 있는가?

첨단 기술 기업가에게 있는 한가지 차이점은 그들은 주식공개상장으로 노다지를 캐는 것이냐 혹은 그들이 다른 곳으로 자리를 뜨기 전에 인수합병을 하느냐 같은 출구전략을 사업 시작 전부터 마음속에 가지고 있다는 것이다. 정반대로 많은 소규모 자영업자들은 단순이 필요에 의해서 그리고 안락한 삶을 살기 위해서 한다. 기업가들은 성공한 그룹에 속해 있다는 점에서 자영업자들과 다른가? 아니면 그저 다른 성공의 정도를 보일 뿐 둘이 똑같은가?

Unit 17. Are you an Entrepreneur?

Key Vocabulary and Phrases

1. Common knowledge
2. Entrepreneur
3. Spot trends
4. Venture capital
5. Angel investor
6. Fund
7. Dormitory
8. Net worth
9. Accuse
10. Cliché
11. Glory
12. Narrative
13. Acumen
14. Execute
15. Self-proclaimed
16. Nerd
17. Start-up
18. Conceivably
19. Attribute
20. To play a part
21. First generation
22. Laid off
23. Conversely
24. Out of necessity
25. IPO
26. M&A

Idioms and Expressions

1. Picking your shots
2. Fall squarely on
3. No such thing as a free lunch
4. Calling the shots
5. Putting everything on the line
6. Bank on it
7. Strike gold
8. Big-league
9. Two peas in a pod

Fill in the blanks with the appropriate word

1. Some __________ in high school became the bosses of those who bullied them later in life.

2. I cringe whenever I hear someone say the old ____________ it's raining cats and dogs.

3. Michael Jordan was a great basketball player but he is also showing his business ______________ as an owner.

4. The person with the highest ______________ in Korea is the chairman of Samsung.

5. The _________________ of a good basketball player are quick feet, large hands, and a good vertical leap.

Match the word with the one that shows its opposite meaning

1. Accuse	**a)** Vindicate
2. Execute	**b)** Jock
3. Nerd	**c)** Similarly
4. Conversely	**d)** Salary man
5. Entrepreneur	**e)** Neglect

Unit 17. Are you an Entrepreneur?

Conversation Questions

1. Why do some nations or regions produce more entrepreneurs?
   What factors lead to an entrepreneurial environment?
2. Is entrepreneurship more about skill or luck? If skill, what kind of skill? If luck, what kind of luck?
3. Where do most entrepreneurs get their ideas?
4. Is it wrong to steal someone's idea and to make a lot of money?
   Would you do it, if given the opportunity?
5. Is it foolish to borrow money from family and friends to start your business?
6. What is the purpose of being an entrepreneur?
   Are the purposes the same in being a small business owner?
7. What are the best industries to start a business in for the next 10–20 years?
8. What traits do entrepreneurs have in common?
9. Is invention born out of necessity or creativity?
10. Who is the most successful entrepreneur or small business owner you personally know?
    How did he/she succeed?

Assignment

Write a sentence using each of the key vocabulary word and idiom given above.

Vocabulary

1.

2.

3.

4.

5.

6.

7.

8.

9.

10.

11.

12.

13.

14.

15.

16.

17.

18.

19.

20.

Unit 17. Are you an Entrepreneur?

21.

22.

23.

24.

25.

26.

Idioms

1.

2.

3.

4.

5.

6.

7.

8.

9.

10.

Class Idea

In groups, make a brief business plan for a business near your school campus. Write a report on the local industry, target market, marketing plan, and the amount of money you need to execute your business strategy successfully.

Explore Further

On YouTube listen to the TED talk by Seth Godin

How to Get Your Ideas to Spread

Definition of Key Words

- **Entrepreneur** n. a person who starts a business and is willing to risk loss in order to make money;
  He was a successful entrepreneur before the age of 25.
  Origin: French, from Old French, first known use in 1852

- **Venture capital** n. money that is used to start a new business;
  Silicon Valley has more venture capital than other places around the world.
  Origin: first known use in 1943

Unit 17. Are you an Entrepreneur?

- **Cliché** n. — a phrase or expression that has been used so often that it is no longer original or interesting; something that is so commonly used in books, stories, etc., that it is no longer effective;
  A speech filled with clichés is really boring to listen to.
  Origin: French, first known use in 1882

- **Narrative** n. — a story that is told or written; *He is writing a detailed narrative of his life on the island.*
  Synonyms: chronicle, chronology, commentary, history, account
  Origin: first known use in 1567

- **Acumen** n. — the ability to think clearly and make good decisions; *Her political acumen won her the election.*
  Synonyms: caginess, astuteness, sharpness, shrewdness, wit
  Origin: Latin, first known use in 1579

- **Execute** v. — to kill someone especially as punishment for a crime;
  He was captured, tried, and executed for murder.
  to do something that you have planned to do or been told to do; to do or perform;
  He executed the business plan perfectly.
  Synonyms: administer, apply, enforce, implement
  Origin: Middle English, from Anglo-French, first known use in the 14th century

- **Converse** v. — to talk usually informally with someone; to have a conversation;
  They conversed quietly in the corner of the room.

- **Converse** n. — something reversed in order, relation, or action

- **Converse** adj. — opposite or reverse; *One must also consider the converse case.*
  Origin: first known use in 1794

pp. 184~189 한국어 해설

당신은 사업가인가?

주요단어 및 구절

1. 상식
2. 기업가
3. 트렌드를 발견하다, 추세를 찾다
4. 벤처자본
5. 선의의 투자자
6. 자금을 대다, 자금을 내다
7. 기숙사
8. 순자산
9. 고발하다, 고소하다
10. 상투적 문구
11. 영광
12. 이야기, 서술, 묘사
13. 감각
14. 실행하다
15. 자칭
16. 괴짜
17. 신생업체, 창업자
18. 상상컨대, 상상할 수 있는
19. 특성, 속성
20. 역할을 하다
21. 1세대
22. 해고된, 해고당한
23. 반대로
24. 필요상, 부득이하게
25. 주식공개상장
26. 인수합병

숙어 및 표현

1. 기회 고르기[는]
2. 어깨 위에 정확히 떨어지다
3. 공짜란 없다
4. 통제하기[는]
5. 모든 것을 걸기[거는]
6. 믿다, 확신하다
7. 노다지를 캐다
8. 성공한 그룹, 큰 물, 큰 리그
9. 같다

빈칸 채우기

1. Nerds
2. Cliché
3. Acumen
4. Net worth
5. Attributes

반대의 의미 단어 찾기

1. a
2. e
3. b
4. c
5. d

대화 질문

1. 왜 어떤 국가나 지역이 더 많은 기업가를 만들어내는가? 어떤 요인이 기업가 환경을 이끄는가?
2. 기업가 정신은 기술이나 행운 쪽 무엇에 가까운가? 만약 기술이라면, 어떤 종류의 기술을 말하는가? 만약 행운이라면, 어떤 종류의 행운을 말하는가?
3. 대부분의 기업가들은 어디에서 아이디어를 얻는가?
4. 남의 아이디어를 훔쳐 많은 돈을 버는 것은 잘못된 것인가? 만약 당신에게 그런 기회가 생긴다면 할 것인가?
5. 사업을 시작하기 위해 가족이나 친구에게 돈을 빌리는 것은 바보 같은 짓인가?
6. 기업가의 목표는 무엇인가? 작은 자영업자의 목표와 똑같은가?
7. 10-20년 후 사업하기 가장 좋은 산업은 어떤 것일까?
8. 기업가가 공통적으로 가지고 있는 특성은 무엇인가?
9. 발명은 필수에 의해 태어나는가 창의성에 의해 태어나는가?
10. 당신이 개인적으로 아는 가장 성공한 기업가 혹은 자영업자는 누구인가? 그/그녀는 어떻게 성공하게 되었는가?

과제

위에 주어진 단어와 숙어를 가지고 문장을 만드시오.

수업 아이디어

그룹별로, 캠퍼스 가까이에서 사업할 간단한 사업 계획서를 만들어 보아라. 당신의 사업 전략을 성공적으로 경영하기 위해 필요한 지역 산업, 목표마켓, 마케팅 계획 그리고 금액을 보고서에 작성하라.

Unit 18

Regions and Clusters

The U.S. has the largest economy in the world, as measured by gross domestic product (GDP) or gross national product (GNP). GDP is the value of all the goods and services produced within a country in a given year, whereas GNP includes all the labor and property owned by citizens abroad. For example, as China's GDP grows, many American companies are benefiting because they have made large foreign direct investments (FDI) in the country. If a country has a robust economy, then its citizens will have jobs to purchase goods and services, which encourage further business activity and investment.

Yet, amidst all the chaos about the national economy, it is regions that make up most economic activities. Essentially, a dozen regions in the U.S. including Northern and Southern California; Boston and Washington; and Dallas and Austin contribute over 70% of the U.S. population as well as producing approximately 75% of all economic activities. That means a region such as Northern California has an economy the same size as Turkey. Or Dallas and Austin's economic output is about the size of oil-rich Saudi Arabia. Likewise, Eastern China including Beijing and Shanghai is disproportionately wealthier than Western China, causing a huge migration of workers to the major cities.

One way to look at it is that regions or clusters have a concentration of businesses, suppliers, and institutes to help them specialize in a certain field, which leads to a competitive advantage over others in the field. For example, Los Angeles is famous for making movies, New York City is famous for fashion, and Silicon Valley is associated with high technology.

Let us examine Silicon Valley. Silicon Valley has a lot of venture capitalists who are eager to hear business ideas, has the world-class universities such as Stanford that produces great people and ideas, and a multitude of firms which locate there to be close to those great people and ideas. As more firms move there, more employees move there and vice versa along with the influx of venture capitalists and scholars who move there to be around great talent.

People make ideas and ideas turn into business opportunities and Silicon Valley is able to choose from the best. Its success has led to a brain drain from across the nation and across the world. Some top sources in talent for Silicon Valley come from Japan, South Korea, China, and India.

Silicon Valley is highly diversified. Since 2010, more Asian Americans are working there than Caucasians. Moreover one-third of the start-ups in Silicon Valley are founded by Indian Americans. Unmistakably, regions benefit from having the right ingredients and make up a large percentage of a nation's growth. Policy planners should focus then on how they can encourage a convergence of firms, talent, and institutions.

In the Bible, Matthew 25:29 states that "For unto every one hath shall be given, and he shall have abundance: but from him that hath not shall be taken even that which he hath." Sociologists have used this verse to explain why "the rich get richer and the poor get poorer." The Matthew Effect refers to the cumulative advantage of economic capital. As Silicon Valley gets more, the more they are able to get. Truth be told, its success is very difficult to replicate. But what are the regions in your country doing to power the economy?

- Key Vocabulary
- Idioms and Expressions

해석

지역과 클러스터

GDP나 GNP로 측정했을 때 미국의 경제는 세계에서 가장 크다. GDP는 1년간 국내에서 생산된 총 재화와 서비스의 가치를 뜻하는 반면, GNP는 해외에 있는 국민들의 모든 노동과 자산을 포함한다. 예를 들어, 중국 GDP가 성장하면 많은 미국 기업들이 중국에 해외 직접 투자를 많이 해왔기 때문에 이익을 본다. 만약 국가가 탄탄한 경제를 가지고 있다면, 그 국민들은 재화와 서비스 구매를 가능하게 하는 직업을 가질 것이고 이는, 더 나은 사업활동이나 투자를 장려한다.

그러나 국가 경제의 혼돈 속에서 대부분의 경제활동은 지방에서 이루어진다. 기본적으로, 남과 북 캘리포니아, 보스턴과 워싱턴, 달라스와 오스틴을 포함하는 미국의 여러 지방들은 미국 인구의 70% 이상과 대략 75%에 달하는 미국 경제활동의 산출에 기여한다. 이것은 북 캘리포니아 같은 지방이 터키와 같은 경제 규모를 가지고 있다는 말이거나, 달라스와 오스틴의 경제 산출량이 석유자원이 풍부한 사우디아라비아와 같다는 의미이다. 비슷하게, 베이징과 상하이를 포함하는 중국 동부는 중국 서부보다 불균형적으로 더 잘 살기 때문에 대도시로 이동하는 대규모의 노동자들이 생기게 한다.

한 가지 관점은 지역이나 클러스터(군집)는 기업들, 공급회사들, 그리고 한 분야의 전문화를 도와주는 기관들이 집중되어 있고, 이는 해당분야에서 다른 지역들보다 경쟁적으로 유리한 이점을 갖게 해 준다. 예를 들어, LA는 영화를 만드는 것으로 유명하고, 뉴욕은 패션으로 유명하며 실리콘 밸리는 첨단산업과 연결되어 있다.

실리콘 밸리를 한번 살펴보자. 실리콘 밸리에는 사업 아이디어를 듣기를 열망하며, 훌륭한 사람들과 아이디어를 생산하는 스탠포드와 같은 세계수준의 대학들을 갖길 원하는 벤처 투자자들이 많이 있다. 그리고 그런 훌륭한 사람들과 아이디어에 근접하기 위해 그곳에 위치한 많은 회사들이 있다. 더 많은 기업들이 그곳으로 옮김으로써, 더 많은 노동자들이 그곳으로 이동한다. 그리고 더 많은 노동자들이 이동함으로써, 훌륭한 인재와 가까이 있으려는 벤처투자자들과 학자들의 유입과 함께 많은 회사들이 그곳으로 이동한다.

사람들은 아이디어를 만들고 아이디어는 사업 기회들이 되며 실리콘 밸리는 최고 중 최고를 뽑을 수 있다. 이것의 성공은 나라 전체 그리고 전 세계에서의 두뇌유출을 이끌어낸다. 실리콘 밸리의 몇몇 최고 재능의 원천은 일본, 한국, 중국 그리고 인도에서 온다.

실리콘 밸리는 매우 다양화되어 있다. 2010년 이후로, 백인보다 더 많은 아시안 아메리칸들이 그곳에서 일을 한다. 게다가 실리콘 밸리의 신생기업 중 3분의 1은 인디안 아메리칸에 의해서 설립되었다. 틀림없이, 지역은 알맞은 요소를 갖는 것으로 이익을 취하고 국가 성장의 대부분을 이룬다. 그렇다면 정책 수립자들은 어떻게 그들이 회사, 재능 그리고 기관들이 한 곳에 집합할 수 있게 장려할 수 있는지에 초점을 맞춰야 한다.

성경의 마태복음 25장 29절에서는 "무릇 있는 자는 받아 풍족하게 되고, 없는 자는 그 있는 것까지 빼앗기리라."라고 쓰여져 있다. 사회학자들은 이 구절을 왜 "부자는 더 부자가 되고, 가난한 사람은 더 가난해지는지" 설명하는데 사용했다. 마태효과는 경제자본의 누적 이익을 나타낸다. 실리콘 밸리가 더 얻을수록, 얻을 수 있는 것은 더 많아진다. 솔직히 말하면, 실리콘 밸리의 성공은 모사하기 힘들다. 그렇지만 당신의 나라에서 지역들이 경제 활성화를 위해 무엇을 하고 있는가?

Unit 18. Regions and Clusters

Key Vocabulary and Phrases

1. GDP
2. GNP
3. Abroad
4. FDI
5. Robust
6. Region
7. Migration
8. Multitude
9. Diversified
10. Network
11. Verse
12. Sociologist
13. Cumulative advantage
14. Competitive advantage
15. Disproportionate

Idioms and Expressions

1. Amidst all the chaos
2. Brain drain
3. The Matthew Effect

Fill in the blanks with the appropriate word

1. America has the largest ________ in the world.

2. Los Angeles, California, is one of the most ________________ cities in America.

3. The coastal areas of China are _________________ wealthier than the western part of China.

4. Silicon Valley is known for its _____________ innovation in the ICT industry.

5. My favorite ______________ in the bible always gives me strength.

Match the word with the one that shows its opposite meaning

1. Diversity	**a)** Sameness
2. Migrate	**b)** Impotent
3. Robust	**c)** Balanced
4. Abroad	**d)** Stay
5. Disproportionate	**e)** National

Unit 18. Regions and Clusters

Conversation Questions

1. What factors make Silicon Valley so successful in terms of economic growth?
2. How does immigration play a role in gaining talent?
3. Does Korea attract highly skilled immigrants?
   What can policy planners do to attract the world's best talent?
4. What other regions in America are powerful drivers of the economy?
5. What regions contribute heavily to economic growth in Korea?
6. What industries are doing the best in powerful regions of the U.S. and Korea?
7. What regions in Korea have lagged behind other regions in development?
   What are the reasons?
8. How do universities, firms, and policy work together to create an explosive business cluster?
9. Is the U.S. uniquely equipped to handle diversity?
   Can Korea also integrate the influx of diverse workers from around the world?
10. What is the role of the world-class university to the development of a region?

Assignment

Write a sentence using each of the key vocabulary word and idiom given above.

Vocabulary

1.
2.
3.
4.
5.
6.
7.
8.
9.
10.
11.
12.
13.
14.
15.

Idioms

1.
2.
3.

Unit 18. Regions and Clusters

Class Idea

As a group, conduct research on what policy planners have done to follow the model of Silicon Valley in Korea. How would you rate their efforts?

Definition of Key Words

- **Abroad** adv. or adj. — in or to a foreign country, going from one person to the next; away from your home;
  I want to study abroad.
  Origin: first known use in the 13th century

- **Robust** adj. — strong and healthy; strongly formed or built;
  successful or impressive and not likely to fall or weaken; *He is in robust health.*
  Synonyms: able-bodied, fit, hearty, healthy, well-conditioned
  Origin: Latin, first known use in 1533

- **Region** n. — a part of a country, of the world, etc. that is different or separate from other parts in some way;
  a place on your body; the parts of a country that are not close to the capital city;
  She has pain in the lower back region.
  Synonyms: area, field, zone
  Origin: Middle English, from Anglo-French, first known use in the 14th century

- **Migration** v. — to move from one country or place to live or work in another; of a bird or animal:
  to move from one area to another at different times of the year;
  He migrates from New York to Florida each winter.
  Origin: Latin, first known use in 1697

- **Diversify** v. — to change something so that it has more different kinds of people or things;
  to produce or sell more kinds of products;
  to increase the variety of goods or services produced or offered by someone or something;
  The company needs to diversify.
  Origin: first known use in the 15th century

- **Network** n. a system of lines, wires, etc., that are connected to each other;
a system of computers and other devices that are connected to each other;
a group of people that are closely connected and that work with each other;
He hooked up his computer to the network.
Origin: first known use in 1535

- **Verse** n. writing in which words are arranged in a rhythmic pattern; a part of a poem or song;
one of the parts of a chapter of the bible; *The epic tale was written in verse.*
Synonyms: lyric, rune, song, poem

- **Verse** v. to familiarize by close association, study, or experience
Origin: Latin, first known use in 1599

- **Sociology** n. the study of society, social institutions, and social relationships;
Sociology may be the broadest social science.
Origin: French, first known use in 1843

- **Disproportionate** adj. having or showing a difference that is not fair, reasonable, or expected;
too large or too small in relation to something;
He believes that middle-class people bear a disproportionate share of the tax burden.
Origin: first known use in 1555

pp. 196~200 한국어 해설

지역과 클러스터

주요단어 및 구절

1. 국내 총생산
2. 국민 총생산
3. 해외에서, 해외로
4. 외국인직접투자
5. 튼튼한, 원기 왕성한
6. 지역, 지방
7. 이주, 이민
8. 다수, 아주 많은 수, 군중
9. 변화가 많은,
   여러 가지의, 다각적인
10. 망, 네트워크
11. 운문, 시
12. 사회학자
13. 누적이익
14. 경쟁우위
15. 불균형의

숙어 및 표현

1. 혼돈 가운데에
2. 두뇌유출
3. 마태효과

빈칸 채우기

1. GDP
2. Diverse
3. Disproportionately
4. Robust
5. Verse

반대의 의미 단어 찾기

1. a
2. d
3. b
4. e
5. c

대화 질문

1. 경제 성장 면에서 어떤 요인이 실리콘 밸리를 매우 성공적으로 만들었는가?
2. 어떻게 이민이 재능을 얻는 역할을 하는가?
3. 한국은 고도로 숙련된 이민자들을 끌어오고 있는가?
   세계 제일의 인재를 끌기 위해 정책 수립자는 어떻게 해야 하는가?
4. 미국의 어떤 다른 지역이 경제에 영향력을 미치는 동인인가?
5. 어떤 지역이 한국의 경제성장에 지대한 기여를 하는가?
6. 한국과 미국의 영향력이 큰 지역에서 최고의 산업은 무엇인가?
7. 한국에서 다른 지역보다 발전에서 뒤쳐진 지역은 어느 지역인가?
   이유는 무엇인가?
8. 대학들, 회사들 그리고 정책이 폭발적인 비즈니스 클러스터를 만들기 위해 어떻게 함께 일해야 하는가?
9. 다양성을 다루기 위해 미국만이 유일하게 잘 갖추어져 있는가?
   한국 또한 세계로부터 다양한 노동자들의 유입을 통합시킬 수 있는가?
10. 지역발전에 세계 수준의 명문대의 역할은 무엇인가?

과제

위에 주어진 단어와 숙어를 가지고 문장을 만드시오.

수업 아이디어

그룹별로, 한국에서 실리콘 밸리를 따라 하기 위해 정책 수립자가 한 일이 무엇인지 조사하시오. 당신이 그들의 노력을 평가한다면?

idioms

A picture is worth a thousand words	천마디 말보다 한번 보는 게 낫다
A rising tide lifts all boats	밀물은 모든 배를 뜨게 만든다
A walk in the park	쉬운
Across the board	전반에 걸쳐서
Actions speak louder than words	백문이 불여일견, 말보다 행동
A different take	다른, 다름
Ahead of the curve	시대에 앞서서, 유행에 앞서서
Aim for the sky	목표를 높게 갖다
All roads lead to Rome/Seoul	모든 길은 로마 / 서울로 연결된다
Amidst all the chaos	혼란인 가운데
Average Joe	평균적인 사람
Bank on it	믿다, 확신하다
Basket case	마비된 것, 머리가 이상한 사람
Benefit of the doubt	선의의 해석, 좋게 봐주다
Big-league	성공한 그룹, 큰 물, 큰 리그
Brain drain	두뇌유출
Break your back	뼈빠지게 일하다
Bringing you down	떨어뜨리는[기], 콧대를 꺾다
Burn out	에너지를 소진하다
Butterflies in your stomach	몹시 긴장하다 (긴장해서 속이 울렁거린다, 긴장해서 가슴이 두근거린다)
Calling the shots	통제하는[기]
Cash cow	고수익 상품
Cold feet	겁, 긴장
Come to grips (with)	이해하다
Common knowledge	상식
Costing an arm and a leg	엄청나게 비싼
Cut from the same cloth	매우 비슷한
Devil's advocate	일부러 반대 입장을 말하다
Diamond in the rough	진흙 속의 다이아몬드
Dime a dozen	매우 흔한, 매우 싼
Don't bite off more than you can chew	감당도 안 될 일을 벌리지 말아라
Easier said than done	행동보다 말이 쉽다, 말이야 쉽다
Eggs in one basket	한가지 일에 모든 것을 걸다
Ends justify the means	모로 가도 서울만 가면 된다
Everything is in the bag	틀림없다, 확실하다
Fair shake at getting ahead	앞으로 나갈 수 있는 공정한 기회
Fall squarely on	어깨 위에 정확히 떨어지다
Fall through the cracks	빠지다
Food for thought	생각해 볼 일, 생각해 볼만한 것
Forking over	넘겨주는[기], 지불하는[기]
Fudge the truth	사실을 날조하다
Getting on someone's nerves	~의 신경을 건드리는[기]
Getting straight to the point	단도직입적인
Good ol' boy network	학연
Half of it is just showing up	절반만이 나타나다
Have the best of both worlds	양 측면을 다 만족시키다

Having a thick skin	철면피를 가지다 – 뻔뻔하다
Having the upper hand	이기다, 우세하다
Hold the key	열쇠를 쥐고 있다
In your own element	자신을 유지하는
It is not rocket science	고도의 지능이 요구되는 일은 아니다
Keeping the eye on the ball	주의를 기울이는[기], 방심하지 않는[기]
Land on your feet	난관을 이겨내다
Learn on the fly	그때그때 배우다
Loose cannon	예측불허의 사람, 돌출행동을 하는 사람
Low-ball offer	낮은 견적 제시
Miss the boat	기회를 놓치다
Monkey wrench	장애물
Night and day	밤낮으로, 전혀
No man is an island	아무도 혼자인 사람은 없다
No such thing as a free lunch	공짜란 없다
On top of it all	게다가
Out of left field	뜻밖에
Out of touch	멀어져서
Pay the price	대가를 치르다
Penny-pinching	구두쇠의, 인색한 (penny-pincher 구두쇠)
Picking your shots	기회를 고르는[기]
Piece of cake	몹시 쉬운 (누워서 떡먹기)
Playing it safe	안전을 기하다
Poker Face	무표정한 얼굴
Pull it off	해내다
Put on your thinking cap	심사숙고하다
Putting everything on the line	모든 것을 걸기[거는]
Rags to riches	무일푼에서 부자로
Safe to say	~라고 해도 괜찮다
Screw up	망치다
Seeing eye to eye	의견이 일치하는[기]
Sharp as a tack	예리한, 머리회전이 빠른
Shedding light on	비추는[기], 해명하는[기], 밝히는[기]
Shed light on something	~을 밝히다, 알려주다
Shoot straight from the hip	솔직하게 말하다, 직설적으로 말하다
Something to chew on	곰곰이 생각할 거리
Stay on top of things	매사에 훤히 알다, 잘 하다
Stick around	머무르다
Straight from the gut	단지 직감으로
Strike gold	노다지를 캐다
Taking the high road	도덕적으로 올바른 태도를 취하다, (싸움) 차분한 태도를 취하다
the bottom line	핵심은, 요점은
the catch is/what's the catch?	속셈은…… / 무슨 속셈이냐?
the clock is ticking	시간이 흘러가다, 시간이 촉박하다
the devil is in the details	악마는 사소한 것 속에 있다
the Matthew Effect	마태효과

Appendix

the name-of-the-game	가장 중요한 것
There are no ifs and buts about it	예외가 없다
Think on your feet	재빨리 대응하다
Think straight	논리적으로 생각하다
Time is money	시간이 돈이다
Trying your luck	되든 안 되든 한번 해보는[기]
Trade-off	균형을 유지하다, 균형
Two peas in a pod	같다
Two sides to a coin	동전의 양면
Upside down day	엉망진창인 날
When the going gets tough, the tough gets going	상황이 힘들어지면 강인한 사람들은 더 강해진다
You can't have your cake and eat it too	케익을 먹고 또 가질 수는 없다 (한가지만 가능하다)
80–20 rule	80–20 법칙 (이탈리아 경제학자 파레토의 원리라고 불리는 법칙 - 20%의 이탈리아 국민들이 국부의 80%를 차지하고 있다)

key words

Abroad	해외에서, 해외로
Abundance	풍부
Accomplish	업적을 이루다, 성취하다
Accumulating	축적하는
Accuse	고발하다, 고소하다
Accustomed	익숙한
Acing a test	시험 만점 받기
Acumen	감각
Adage	속담
Admiration	감탄, 존경
Adopt	받아들이다, 택하다
Advice	충고
Aim	목표
Alert	초롱초롱한, 생기 있는
Ambition	포부
American Dream	아메리칸 드림 (미국에 가면 무슨 일을 하든 행복하게 잘살 수 있으리라는 생각)
Anchoring principle	정착이론
An edge	우세함 / 유리함
Angel investor	선의의 투자자
Anticipate	예상하다
Aptitude	소질
Ardent	열렬한
Arrogant	오만한
Arsenal	비축, 무기
Aspiring	떠오르는, 야심에 찬
Attainable	달성할 수 있는
Attribute	특성, 속성
Being a Santa Claus	산타클로스가 되는 것
Big deal	큰 일, 대단한 것
Big fish in a small pond/Small fish in a big pond	뱀의 머리 / 용의 꼬리
Billionaire	억만장자
Bloomberg	블룸버그 회사
Bombarded	공세를 받는, 퍼부어지는
Bond	맺다
Bully	깡패
Bump	튀어나온, 오르다, 격상
Captivate	마음을 사로잡다
Category	분류
Character	성품, 개성
Charity	자선단체, 자선
Chronological	순서대로
Circumstances	환경
Clear no-no	하면 정말 안 되는 행동
Cliché	상투적 문구
Clutter	채우다, 잡동사니
Colleague	동료
Common knowledge	상식
Competitive advantage	경쟁이익
Conceivably	상상컨대, 상상할 수 있는
Confidence	자신감
Conflict	갈등
Connection	연결, 관련성
Conservative	보수적인
Conservative	보수적인
Considerate	배려하는, 사려깊은
Consistent	한결같은, 일치하는
Contemporary	동시대인(人), 동시대의
Contention	논쟁, 언쟁
Conversationalist	대화에 능한 사람
Conversely	반대로
Cramming	벼락치기
Credential	증명서, 자격을 수여하다
Crippling	심각한 손상, 마비시키는
Critical	중요한
Criticism	비판
Critic	비평가, 비판가
Crucial	중요한
Cumulative advantage	누적이익
Deadline	마감기한
Debt	빚, 부채
Delay	지연, 연기하다
Deliver	전달하다
Democracy	민주주의
Desire	열정 / 욕망
Disappointed	실망한
Disproportionate	불균형의

Distinguished	구별되는
Distracted	산만한
Divergence	차이
Diversified	변화가 많은, 여러 가지의, 다각적인
Dominance	권력
Dormitory	기숙사
Dropout	중퇴자, 중퇴
Ego	자부심
Eliminate	제거하다
Elite	엘리트, 일류의, 우수한
Embrace	받아들이다
Empathy	감정이입, 공감
Endorphin	엔도르핀
Entangled	얽힌
Enthusiasm	열정
Enthusiastic	열렬한, 열심인
Enticing	매혹적인, 매력적인
Entrepreneur	기업가
Envy	부러움
Escort	호위하다, 호위
Essential	필수적인
Etiquette	예의, 예절
Evident	분명한, 눈에 띄는
Exaggerate	과장하다
Execute	실행하다
Exemplary	모범적인
Exert	행사하다, 가하다
Exert	노력하다, 분투하다
Exhaustive	총망라한, (빠뜨리는 것 없이) 철저한
Expectation	예상, 기대
Experienced	경험이 있는, 노련한
Extravagant	낭비하는, 사치스러운
Fair	공평한, 타당한
Faith	믿음, 신뢰
Fast track	출세가도, 빠른 출세길
Favor	부탁
FDI	외국인직접투자
Feedback loop	피드백 순환
Figure	판단하다
Fine print	세세한 항목
First generation	1세대
Flock	모이다
Fluent	능숙한 / 유창한
Focus	집중하다, 초점을 맞추다
Fortune	재산, 부, 행운
Fret	조마조마하다
Fringe benefits	부가혜택
Frugality	절약, 검소
Functional	기능적인
GDP	국내 총생산
Geek	괴짜
Generalization	일반화
Genuinely	진정으로
Getting the message across	메시지를 전달하는
Getting with the program	태도를 바꾸어 할 일을 하기[는]
Gift of gab	말솜씨
Give and take	타협, 교환, 주고 받다
Globalization	세계화
Glory	영광
GNP	국민 총생산
Go for it	시도하다
Goals	목표
Go-getter	성공하려고 단단히 작정한
Goodwill	호의
Gossip	소문, 험담
Gratification	희열, 만족감
Guide	인도하다
Hallmark	특징
Hardwired	타고난, 선천적인
Heir	상속인
Hierarchy	우선순위 / 계급
High capacity	고성능, 높은 능력
High-context culture	고 맥락 문화
Highlight	강조하다
Highly self-monitoring	고도의 자기점검
Hot job	유망직종
Hot seat	어려운 상황에 처한
Humiliation	창피함, 굴욕
Hunch	예감, 감
Immense	엄청난
Immense	엄청난
Imposing	인상적인
In all likelihood	십중팔구
In the long run	장기에는
Inclined	하고 싶은, 마음이 기울다
Income-based repayment	소득기준상환
Industry	산업
Ineligible	부적격의
Inequality of wealth	부의 불평등
Inevitable bumps	피할 수 없는 방지 턱
Infectious	전염되는
Infinite	무한의, 끝없는
Influence	영향
Initiative	결단력
Innovation	혁신
Instinct	직감, 본능
Insult	모욕하다
Interdependency	상호의존
Interrupt	방해하다, 중단시키다
Intuition	직관, 직관력, 직감

Invariably	변함없이	Oligarchy	과두정부
Invisible	눈에 보이지 않는	On-site	현장의, 공동의
IPO	주식공개상장	Open up the doors...	기회를 주다
Just get by	그럭저럭 지내다	Optimistic	낙천적인 / 낙관적인
Killer	죽이는 / 죽여주는	Ostensible	표면적으로는
Knowledge for the sake of knowledge	지식을 위한 지식	Out of necessity	필요상, 부득이하게
		Outlier	큰 성공을 거둔 사람, 표본들 중 다른 대상들과 확연히 구분되는 것
Label	탁지를 붙이다, 꼬리표를 붙이다		
Labor market	노동시장	Output	결과, 생산량
Lag	뒤처지다	Overseas	해외의
Laid off	해고된, 해고당한	Paralyzing	끔찍한
Late bloomer	대기만성, 늦깍이	Particular	특별한
Lazy	게으른	Passion	열정
Leadership	리더십	Passion	열정
Leaning	성향	Pattern-matching machines	패턴 맞추기 기계
Liberal	진보적인, 자유민주적인	Perennial	영원한
Low-context culture	저 맥락 문화	Persuade	설득하다
M&A	인수합병	Pertinent	적절한 / 관련된
Make it on their own	스스로 헤쳐나가다	Peruse	정독하다
Management	경영	Phenomenon	현상
Mandatory	의무적인	Philanthropy	자선활동, 자선사업
Manifest	나타내다, 분명해지다	Plotting	음모, 계획
Maternity leave	출산휴가	Policy	정책
Measured	측정된 / 측정한	Ponder	심사숙고 하다
Media	미디어, 대중매체	Positive energy	긍정적 에너지
Meritocracy	실력주의	Posture	자세
Middle class	중산층 (middle-class 중산층의)	Poverty	가난, 빈곤
Migration	이주, 이민	Predisposition	성향, 경향
Millennials	수천 년	Premium	고급의
Millionaire	백만장자	Presence	존재하다, 있음, 현장감
Multitude	다수, 아주 많은 수, 군중	Prestige	명문, 명성
Mutually beneficial	상호이익의	Prioritize	우선순위를 매기다
Myers-Briggs test	마이어브릭스 테스트	Procrastination	연기, 지연, 꾸물거림
Narrative	이야기, 서술, 묘사	Professional	전문적인
Navigate	길을 찾다	Proficient	능숙한
Navigating	길을 찾는	Pronounced	확연한, 단호한
Naysayer	반대론자, 비관론자	Protruding	튀어나오다
Negotiation	협상	Publicity	선전, 광고
Nerd	괴짜	Put off until the last minute	마지막 순간까지 미루다
Net worth	순자산	Quantifiable	수량화할 수 있는
Network	망, 네트워크	Radically	급진적으로
Never failing to deliver	전달하는데 절대 실패하지 않다	Rally behind	지지하다
No-brainer	쉬운 문제	Ranking	순서, 랭킹
Not take things personal	기분 나쁘게 받아들이지 않다	Rapidly	빨리, 급격히
Novice	초보자	Rapper	래퍼, 랩 가수
Obsessed	사로잡히다, 집착하다	Reasoning	추리, 추론, 논리
Obstacle	장애물	Reference	추천인
Oddball	괴짜	Refine	개선하다
OECD	경제협력개발기구	Regions	지역, 지방
Offset	상쇄하다	Rehearse	예행연습(하다)

Reimbursement	상환
Reputation	평판
Rerun	재방송
Resilience	회복력
Resolve	결의, 해결하다
Resort	행사하다, 호소하다
Respect	존경
Retain	유지하다
Retaliation	보복
Revise	수정하다, 검토하다
Reward	보상
Robust	튼튼한, 원기 왕성한
Rough	거친
Rumor	소문
Sacrifice	희생
SAT	(미국)대학수능시험
Savvy	지식
Scenario	시나리오
Scrambling	서둘러, 무질서한
Scrutinize	세심히 살피다 / 보다
Self-aware	자기인식, 자각
Self-made	자수성가한
Self-proclaimed	자칭
Sense of urgency	절박감
Shame	수치심, 부끄러움
Sheer	순전한, 완전히
Single-parent home	편부모 가정
Sloppy	엉성한
Slouch	구부정한
Sociologists	사회학자
Solution	해결책, 해답
Spectator	관중
Spot trends	트렌드를 발견하다, 추세를 찾다
Stable	안정된, 안정적인
Standard	보통의, 표준의
Staring	응시하는
Start-up	신생업체, 창업자
Starving Artist	예술을 위해 돈을 포기한 예술가
Stellar	뛰어난, 별의
Stereotype	선입견, 고정관념, 편견
Stew	화를 내다, 속을 태우다
Stick around	머무르다
Store	저장하다
Strategy	전략
Striking	눈에 띄는, 현저한, 인상적인
Student syndrome	학생 증후군
Subconscious	잠재의식
Sub-par	보통 이하의
Sunken Costs Fallacy	매몰비용 오류
Supremely	극도로, 지극히
System	시스템
Tailor	교정하다
Tandem	2인용 자전거, 앞뒤 한 줄로, 나란한(in tandem ~와 동시에)
Tangible and intangible	유형 무형의
Tenure	재임기간
Thick skin	철면피
Thrive	성공하다
Titans	거물, 거인
to feel sorry for yourself	한탄하다
to fund	자금을 대다, 자금을 내다
to get in on the action	편승하다, 끼어들다
to heed	주의를 기울이다
to play a part	역할을 하다
to standout	눈에 띄다
To-do list	해야 할 일 목록
Too bad	애석한
Touch the lives of those around us	주변 사람들과 관련이 있다, 주변 사람들에게 영향을 미치다
Tuck	집어넣다
Tycoon	거물, 재벌
Ubiquitous	어디에나 있는, 아주 흔한
Ultimately	결국, 궁극적으로, 근본적으로
Unambiguous	명백한
Uncouth	보기흉한
Understated	과소평가된, 무시된
Until the last minute	마지막 순간까지
Upper crust	상류층
Vanguard	선두, 선봉
Venture capital	벤처자본
Verse	운문, 시
Vibe	분위기
Visible	눈에 보이는 / 가시적인
Wacky	괴짜의, 터무니 없는
Well-calculated risks	면밀이 계획된 위험
Winging it	임기응변하다
Win-win situation	윈윈 상황
Wired	연결된
Wither	시들다, 약해지다
Without a doubt	틀림없이, 의심할 여지 없이
Wrong to lie on principle	거짓말 하는 것은 도덕상 옳지 않은
You better believe ...	…이 틀림없다

Business English Now!

2015년 2월 10일 초판 인쇄
2015년 2월 25일 초판 발행

저 자 Alex Timberman
발행인 배 효 선
발행처 法 文 社

주 소 경기도 파주시 회동길 37-29 (문발동)
등 록 1957. 12. 12. / 제2-76호(윤)
Tel 031-955-6500 Fax 031-955-6525
e-mail (영업) bms@bobmunsa.co.kr
(편집) edit66@bobmunsa.co.kr
홈페이지 http: //www.bobmunsa.co.kr
조판 법 문 사 전 산 실

정가 17,000원 ISBN 978-89-18-51347-8